T0146974

MACAT

An Analysis of

James Ferguson's

The Anti-Politics Machine

"Development," Depoliticization, and Bureaucratic Power in Lesotho

Julie Jenkins

ROUTLEDGE

Published by Macat International Ltd
24:13 Coda Centre, 189 Munster Road, London SW6 6AW.

Distributed exclusively by Routledge
2 Park Square, Milton Park, Abingdon, Oxon OX14 4RN
711 Third Avenue, New York, NY 10017, USA

Routledge is an imprint of the Taylor & Francis Group, an informa business

www.macat.com
info@macat.com

Cataloguing in Publication Data
A catalogue record for this book is available from the British Library.
Library of Congress Cataloguing-in-Publication Data is available upon request.
Cover illustration: Etienne Gilfillan

ISBN 978-1-912302-05-5 (hardback)
ISBN 978-1-912128-60-0 (paperback)
ISBN 978-1-912128-30-3 (e-book)

Notice
The information in this book is designed to orientate readers of the work under analysis,
to elucidate and contextualise its key ideas and themes, and to aid in the development
of critical thinking skills. It is not meant to be used, nor should it be used, as a
substitute for original thinking or in place of original writing or research. References and
notes are provided for informational purposes and their presence does not constitute
endorsement of the information or opinions therein. This book is presented solely for
educational purposes. It is sold on the understanding that the publisher is not engaged
to provide any scholarly advice. The publisher has made every effort to ensure that
this book is accurate and up-to-date, but makes no warranties or representations with
regard to the completeness or reliability of the information it contains. The information
and the opinions provided herein are not guaranteed or warranted to produce particular
results and may not be suitable for students of every ability. The publisher shall not be
liable for any loss, damage or disruption arising from any errors or omissions, or from
the use of this book, including, but not limited to, special, incidental, consequential or
other damages caused, or alleged to have been caused, directly or indirectly, by the
information contained within.

CONTENTS

THE MACAT LIBRARY

The Macat Library is a series of unique academic explorations of seminal works in the humanities and social sciences – books and papers that have had a significant and widely recognised impact on their disciplines. It has been created to serve as much more than just a summary of what lies between the covers of a great book. It illuminates and explores the influences on, ideas of, and impact of that book. Our goal is to offer a learning resource that encourages critical thinking and fosters a better, deeper understanding of important ideas.

Each publication is divided into three Sections: Influences, Ideas, and Impact. Each Section has four Modules. These explore every important facet of the work, and the responses to it.

This Section-Module structure makes a Macat Library book easy to use, but it has another important feature. Because each Macat book is written to the same format, it is possible (and encouraged!) to cross-reference multiple Macat books along the same lines of inquiry or research. This allows the reader to open up interesting interdisciplinary pathways.

To further aid your reading, lists of glossary terms and people mentioned are included at the end of this book (these are indicated by an asterisk [*] throughout) – as well as a list of works cited.

Macat has worked with the University of Cambridge to identify the elements of critical thinking and understand the ways in which six different skills combine to enable effective thinking.
Three allow us to fully understand a problem; three more give us the tools to solve it. Together, these six skills make up the **PACIER** model of critical thinking. They are:

ANALYSIS – understanding how an argument is built
EVALUATION – exploring the strengths and weaknesses of an argument
INTERPRETATION – understanding issues of meaning

CREATIVE THINKING – coming up with new ideas and fresh connections
PROBLEM-SOLVING – producing strong solutions
REASONING – creating strong arguments

To find out more, visit **WWW.MACAT.COM.**

CRITICAL THINKING AND *THE ANTI-POLITICS MACHINE*

Primary critical thinking skill: CREATIVE THINKING
Secondary critical thinking skill: ANALYSIS

James Ferguson's 1990 study *The Anti-Politics Machine* was a radical intervention in development studies that remains influential in the field today. It is also an excellent example of the way in which creative thinking can help shake up an idea, and show problems in a new light. Ferguson's interest was development strategies in the Third World – the interventions by which aid agencies, NGOs and individual countries try to raise poor areas or countries' economic and living standards. Embedded in the community in Lesotho (a small country in southern Africa), Ferguson noted that, time and time again, the same strategies were used by agencies and foreign powers, despite the fact that they had failed many times before.

Seeking to analyse the implications of this discovery, Ferguson made a move that is often employed by creative thinkers: he stepped outside of the standard interpretative framework, and applied a novel way of interpreting the problem. In this case, Ferguson imported his framework and methodology from the French philosopher and historian Michel Foucault, whose theories of power dynamics enabled Ferguson to see the failed development strategies from an entirely new perspective. It is a simple but impactful move that helped revolutionise the discussion.

ABOUT THE AUTHOR OF THE ORIGINAL WORK

While studying at Harvard for his PhD, American anthropologist **James Ferguson** traveled to Lesotho, in southern Africa. He spent 15 months there researching a community that was the subject of a large, international development program at the time. This research formed the basis of his first book, 1990's *The Anti-Politics Machine*, which explores the reasons why technologically based development projects continue to be implemented, despite overwhelmingly failing to alleviate poverty. Ferguson is now a professor of anthropology at Stanford University, and his ideas still have an important influence on those studying international development today.

ABOUT THE AUTHOR OF THE ANALYSIS

Dr Julie Jenkins holds an MSc in anthropology and development from the London School of Economics and a PhD in social anthropology from the University of Sussex. She has been a visiting professor at Ball State University and Washington & Lee University, teaching courses on globalization and international development.

ABOUT MACAT

GREAT WORKS FOR CRITICAL THINKING

Macat is focused on making the ideas of the world's great thinkers accessible and comprehensible to everybody, everywhere, in ways that promote the development of enhanced critical thinking skills.

It works with leading academics from the world's top universities to produce new analyses that focus on the ideas and the impact of the most influential works ever written across a wide variety of academic disciplines. Each of the works that sit at the heart of its growing library is an enduring example of great thinking. But by setting them in context – and looking at the influences that shaped their authors, as well as the responses they provoked – Macat encourages readers to look at these classics and game-changers with fresh eyes. Readers learn to think, engage and challenge their ideas, rather than simply accepting them.

'Macat offers an amazing first-of-its-kind tool for interdisciplinary learning and research. Its focus on works that transformed their disciplines and its rigorous approach, drawing on the world's leading experts and educational institutions, opens up a world-class education to anyone.'

Andreas Schleicher
Director for Education and Skills, Organisation for Economic
Co-operation and Development

'Macat is taking on some of the major challenges in university education ... They have drawn together a strong team of active academics who are producing teaching materials that are novel in the breadth of their approach.'

Prof Lord Broers,
former Vice-Chancellor of the University of Cambridge

'The Macat vision is exceptionally exciting. It focuses upon new modes of learning which analyse and explain seminal texts which have profoundly influenced world thinking and so social and economic development. It promotes the kind of critical thinking which is essential for any society and economy. This is the learning of the future.'

Rt Hon Charles Clarke, former UK Secretary of State for Education

'The Macat analyses provide immediate access to the critical conversation surrounding the books that have shaped their respective discipline, which will make them an invaluable resource to all of those, students and teachers, working in the field.'

Professor William Tronzo, University of California at San Diego

WAYS IN TO THE TEXT

KEY POINTS

- James Ferguson is a cultural anthropologist:* a scholar of human behavior and thought across different cultures.

- In his book *The Anti-Politics Machine*, Ferguson examines the idea of "development"—social and economic change, directed by non-governmental organizations,* and organizations that administer financial aid—and how it is achieved through development interventions. His work has influenced the ways in which present academics in the field are examining development.

- *The Anti-Politics Machine* draws on fieldwork that Ferguson carried out in Lesotho,* a mountainous country surrounded by South Africa, between September 1982 and December 1983.

Who Is James Ferguson?

James Ferguson, the author of *The Anti-Politics Machine* (1990), is an American cultural anthropologist. He was born in 1959 in Los Angeles, California and completed his undergraduate degree at the University of California in Santa Barbara. It was here that he first studied cultural anthropology: the cross–cultural study of human behavior and human thought. After graduating in 1979, Ferguson went on to study social anthropology* at Harvard University, completing his MA in 1981 and his PhD in 1985. After finishing his studies Ferguson taught at the University of California in Irvine from 1986 to 2003, before moving to Stanford University, where he is still a professor.

During his studies Ferguson became interested in the continuing struggles against colonialism* in southern Africa (that is, struggles against the economic and political control of southern African nations by European nations). He planned to carry out research for his PhD in Zimbabwe or Mozambique, countries that had both recently gained independence (Mozambique in 1975 and Zimbabwe in 1980). But Ferguson's thesis advisor suggested that he should go to Lesotho. This landlocked, mountainous country, encircled by South Africa, had gained independence in 1966. Much of its population of 1.3 million lived in poverty. At the time Ferguson was doing his PhD, the World Bank* and the Canadian International Development Agency*— international institutions founded to help "developing" nations through loans (World Bank) or financial aid (CIDA)—had set up a large development* project in Lesotho to try to alleviate the nation's economic problems. In September 1982, Ferguson traveled out to the Thaba-Tseka District to start 15 months of fieldwork. His research would form the basis of his PhD and his influential first book, *The Anti-Politics Machine: "Development," Depoliticization, and Bureaucratic Power in Lesotho,* published in 1990.

What Does *The Anti-Politics Machine* Say?

In *The Anti-Politics Machine,* James Ferguson examines development interventions in Lesotho between 1975 and 1984 and offers a critical analysis of the concept and practice of development. He examines what governments and agencies mean when they talk about "developing" a country. In *The Anti-Politics Machine* Ferguson explores how governments and agencies use development projects to try to achieve their goal of encouraging social and economic change, in the belief that this will increase economic growth and living standards.

The Anti-Politics Machine is based on the fieldwork that Ferguson carried out in Lesotho between 1982 and 1983. He used the anthropological technique of participant observation,* which allows anthropologists to take part in the daily lives of research participants. By doing this Ferguson was able to see how development institutions put the idea of development into practice and to examine the effects of the project on the local population.

One of the issues raised in *The Anti-Politics Machine* is that, although development projects have a high rate of failure when it comes to reducing poverty and economic inequality, similar approaches are used time and again. Ferguson says that while development institutions produce knowledge about the conditions and causes of poverty, they fail to acknowledge many of the historical or political factors that are also related to poverty. As a result, the facts produced by development institutions do not accurately describe matters on the ground, but do show the priorities and assumptions of development agencies.

The key problem with development knowledge for Ferguson is the way that it "depoliticizes"* poverty. He argues that development practitioners see poverty in terms of resources and technology. As a result, the focus of development becomes the provision of technical solutions: improved agricultural techniques, water supplies, transport links. But this ignores the bigger picture: the reality that political action also shapes the existence and experience of poverty within a country. Ferguson calls development the "anti-politics machine" because of this blinkered focus on the technical aspects of poverty.

Ferguson's book combines the insights of the influential French philosopher and historian Michel Foucault* with the study of international development. Michel Foucault examined power relations in society. He was interested in the relationship between language, knowledge, and power, arguing that what we think we know as absolute truth is always shaped by power relations. In *The Anti-Politics Machine* Ferguson shows how development agencies produce a specific kind of knowledge about "developing countries." When translated into action, this knowledge can have unintended effects that do not correspond to the project's stated goals. This idea is one of the reasons why Ferguson's text is so influential.

The Anti-Politics Machine has raised awareness of how development knowledge is generated and of the political causes of poverty. It has influenced the work of later academics on international development projects and organizations. And it has been cited over 4,000 times since its publication. Twenty-five years on, anthropologists still regard Ferguson's text as a crucial work in the field of international development.

Why Does *The Anti-Politics Machine* Matter?

Development aims to increase the living standards of the impoverished through social and economic change. The development industry consists largely of non-governmental organizations (NGOs). These are not-for-profit organizations that are not part of a government, but NGOs may be *funded* by governments, as well as by private individuals, businesses, and foundations. The development industry is also made up of bilateral aid organizations, such as the United States Agency for International Development.* In addition, the industry is supported by multilateral* institutions (institutions with a number of member countries) like the World Bank, which provide loans. All these development organizations are united in the goal to eliminate poverty, hunger, lack of shelter, and unnecessary disease. The United Nations,* an international body founded to promote cooperation between the world's nations, most recently reiterated these in its Sustainable Development Goals* of 2015. These goals acknowledge the need to address climate change and promote development, consumption, and production that can continue without seriously compromising the environment. Yet, despite the monetary, technological, and intellectual resources invested in eliminating poverty, the World Bank estimates that 2.2 billion people worldwide live on less than two dollars a day.[1]

The Anti-Politics Machine challenges the way we understand international development and encourages readers to examine the type of knowledge that development experts and planners generate. Ferguson argues that development knowledge creates a particular framework by which to understand the reality of poverty and inequality. This influences how these projects are implemented and can be problematic. This is particularly evident in their emphasis on technical solutions that do not acknowledge the historical and political aspects of poverty. Ferguson points out that development projects can be ineffective in achieving the goal of reducing poverty. However, when development knowledge is translated into action, it can produce several unintended outcomes—including the strengthening of state power and control over citizens.

The book is crucial reading for anyone with an interest in international development. While Ferguson offers no solutions about how to improve development, his insights encourage his readers to reflect on what values and ideas are contained in their field of work. He reminds his readers that poverty is not only about a country's lack of technological or environmental resources. Poverty also has political dimensions, causes, and potential solutions—economic growth does not ensure, for example, that all can equally share access to, or the benefits of, that growth.

NOTES

1   "Overview of Poverty," World Bank, accessed September 16, 2015, http://www.worldbank.org/en/topic/poverty/overview.

SECTION 1
INFLUENCES

THE AUTHOR AND THE HISTORICAL CONTEXT

KEY POINTS

- James Ferguson's book *The Anti-Politics Machine* (1990) is one of the most influential books in the anthropological* study of international development*—planned and directed social and economic change at the national level. An anthropologist is someone engaged in the systematic study of human belief and practices.

- In the book, Ferguson applies the insights of the French philosopher and historian Michel Foucault* to development. Foucault was interested in the concept of power: where power lies, how it is used, and how others respond to it.

- Ferguson wrote the book in the 1980s, when academics and policymakers were starting to ask why development interventions were failing to reduce poverty.

Why Read This Text?

James Ferguson's book *The Anti-Politics Machine: "Development," Depoliticization, and Bureaucratic Power in Lesotho* was published in 1990. In it, Ferguson challenges his readers to examine what is meant by the term "development." What assumptions about the world does "development" entail?

According to Ferguson, even though these were relatively new questions when the book was published, development was, nevertheless, being implemented in communities across the world. As Ferguson argues in the book, "wars are fought and coups launched in its name. Entire systems of government and philosophy are evaluated

> ❝ And my advisor said, 'Well, if you're going to scope out these sites in Southern Africa anyway, why don't you also go to Lesotho.' And I said, 'Well I'm not really interested in Lesotho'. And he said, 'Well, but it's a nice place and you won't get malaria because it's in the mountains and, you know, why don't you go there?' I ended up going. ❞
>
> James Ferguson, "James Ferguson on Modernity, Development, and Reading Foucault in Lesotho," *Theory Talks*

according to their ability to promote it. Indeed, it seems increasingly difficult to find any way to talk about large parts of the world except in these terms."[1]

In *The Anti-Politics Machine* Ferguson, an anthropologist himself, changed the way that anthropologists in general thought about international development institutions and programs. His key contribution was to adopt Michel Foucault's insights into the nature of power. Foucault was an important French philosopher and historian. He had written about different forms of power within society and looked at the relationships between power and the individual. Ferguson's approach to development combines anthropological research methods with an awareness of how power affects societies. He looks at what information feeds into decisions about development; how decisions about development are made; and how they are translated into everyday action. His conclusions challenged the process of international development, and revealed that the *actual* outcomes of development may be very different from the *intended* outcomes. His work in the African country of Lesotho*—a relatively small nation surrounded by South Africa—has inspired other academics to take a critical look at development outcomes elsewhere in the world.

Author's Life

James Ferguson was born in 1959 in Los Angeles, California. He first began studying cultural anthropology* (the cross-cultural study of human behavior and thought) as an undergraduate at the University of California in Santa Barbara. He attributes his initial interest in Africa and development to his teachers at the university, the South African anthropologist David Brokensha* and the American anthropologist Paul Bohannan.*[2] Ferguson went on to take an MA in anthropology* at Harvard University, and then a PhD.

It was in order to carry out research for his PhD that Ferguson first went to Lesotho. Funded by the Social Science Research Council, the American Council of Learned Societies, and a Fulbright Grant,[3] Ferguson went to the Thaba-Tseka District of Lesotho in 1982. He stayed there until 1983.[4]

Two years later, Ferguson completed his PhD and, shortly after, started teaching anthropology at the University of California in Irvine, and intermittently at Harvard University and the University of Michigan. *The Anti-Politics Machine*, based on the research he had carried out in Lesotho, was published in 1990. Thirteen years later, in 2003, Ferguson took an appointment at Stanford University, acting as chair of the anthropology department from 2007 to 2013. He still teaches at Stanford and is married to another anthropologist at the university, Liisa Malkki.*

Author's Background

It was while doing his undergraduate degree that Ferguson became interested in the struggles against colonialism* in southern Africa; white Europeans had settled across much of this region, exploiting the local mineral resources and agricultural opportunities. In order to gain and maintain control over indigenous populations, they established political and economic systems that excluded non-whites. In the late 1970s, some countries were still under the control of these settler populations, who retained a monopoly over political participation and over economic and social resources. Anthropologists had not written extensively about southern African in the context of independence movements and postcolonial* state relations. Ferguson wanted to fill this gap in the existing literature.[5]

Ferguson had initially planned to conduct his research in the southern African nations of Zimbabwe or Mozambique, but his first thesis advisor suggested he should do his research in Lesotho.[6] This mountainous country had become a British colony in 1884, gaining independence in 1966. Since then the population of 1.3 million had been ruled by the Basotho National Party* (BNP).[7] But following the 1970 elections, the BNP's leadership was contested. The party responded by declaring a state of emergency and elections would not be held again until 1993. So, in the 1980s, when Ferguson was carrying out his research for *The Anti-Politics Machine*, Lesotho was ruled by an authoritarian* regime (that is, a government whose intrusive authority restricted the freedoms of its citizens).

This was also the time when people were starting to ask why development projects around the world were failing to increase living standards. Ferguson points out that Lesotho had received a "disproportionate volume of aid" from the mid-1970s to the mid-1980s.[8] But much of this aid was directed towards projects to improve the agricultural base of Lesotho when only 10 percent of the land is arable; the rest is only suitable for grazing livestock.[9] These environmental conditions helped to explain why the projects consistently failed to achieve their objectives.[10] Ferguson asks why the same kinds of project kept being undertaken despite this history of failure.

NOTES

1   James Ferguson, *The Anti-Politics Machine: "Development," Depoliticization, and Bureaucratic Power in Lesotho* (Minneapolis, MN: University of Minnesota Press, 1994), XIII.

2   Ferguson, *The Anti-Politics Machine*, IX; "Theory Talk #34: *James Ferguson on Modernity, Development, and Reading Foucault in Lesotho*," Theory Talks, accessed September 16, 2015, http://www.theory-talks.org/2009/11/theory-talk-34.html.

3   Ferguson, *The Anti-Politics Machine*, IX, VIII.

4   Ferguson, *The Anti-Politics Machine*, VIII.

5   "Theory Talk #34."

6   "Theory Talk #34."

7   Ferguson, *The Anti-Politics Machine*, 3.

8   Ferguson, *The Anti-Politics Machine*, 7.

9   Ferguson, *The Anti-Politics Machine*, 3.

10 Ferguson, *The Anti-Politics Machine*, 8.

MODULE 2
ACADEMIC CONTEXT

KEY POINTS

- Development*—social and economic change, directed by NGOs* and aid organizations—and the processes of social change have always been of interest to anthropologists* (those who study the beliefs and practices of human beings).

- The French philosopher and historian Michel Foucault* challenged the idea that anyone (including anthropologists) could claim that their thinking was objective and scientifically neutral.

- Ferguson was influenced by Foucault's ideas about knowledge and language and what it is (and is not) acceptable to say as a professional working with a particular field.

The Work in its Context

In *The Anti-Politics Machine: "Development," Depoliticization, and Bureaucratic Power in Lesotho*, the anthropologist James Ferguson examines, in-depth, a development intervention in the mountainous southern African nation of Lesotho* from 1975 to 1984. He uses this study to offer a critique of international development.

Ferguson's decision to study a development intervention at a specific historical moment represents a larger theoretical shift in the field of anthropology.* Previous generations of anthropologists— especially those working within the context of European colonial* occupation and exploitation in Africa—neglected to account fully for the colonial experience of some African societies. Their relationship to colonial exploitation had been largely overlooked, as had one key

> ❝ One question anthropologists are sometimes asked by other social scientists is: 'What's the point of all these cases unless we can make generalizations about them?' My starting point is rather different. I would follow Max Weber, and say, on the contrary: 'What's the point of generalizations unless they help us to understand what's right in front of us with these cases?' That is, generalizations are useful when they help us understand that which we encounter, which is always the particular, which is always the world that we live in. ❞
>
> James Ferguson, "James Ferguson on Modernity, Development, and Reading Foucault in Lesotho," *Theory Talks*

response to colonialism: the formation of liberation movements. In addition, little attention had been paid to postcolonial* state relationships. Instead they approached their studies as if they were trying to uncover the logic of a culture prior to colonial intervention. This conceptual framework assumed that culture exists in isolation from outside influences. It also assumed that this culture was fixed and unchanging, with rules and logic continuously reproduced, before being disrupted by colonialism.

Those who criticized this approach questioned the supposed isolation of pre-colonial African cultures. They highlighted the cross-cultural regional and transregional exchanges that had been in place before the arrival of the Europeans. These interactions were important to the process of social change. They helped to produce the cultural context that anthropologists were examining. Inspired by this critique, Ferguson wanted to study the interplay between local experience in Lesotho and what was happening on the wider political stage. The focus for his research was the relationship between international funded development projects and the local realities in Lesotho.

Overview of the Field

By the 1980s, a big shift was taking place in anthropological thinking. Earlier generations of anthropologists had been influenced by structuralist* and structural-functionalist* theories. Structuralist theories argued that the same underlying units or structures of culture (legal systems, for example) could be found in all societies, and that these could be identified through objective analysis. According to structural-functionalist theories, meanwhile, these underlying units or structures also have a common function: they exist to maintain group cohesion and order. During the 1970s and the 1980s, these ideas were being critiqued for lacking historical understanding of social exchange and change. It was also argued that these theories suggest that everyone within a culture shares the same values, interests, and understanding of the world in which they live.

Poststructuralists,* like the French philosopher Michel Foucault, were critical of these theories. Within anthropology, both poststructuralist and feminist* anthropologists started to argue that there are multiple meanings and interpretations of the structures within any given society (feminism, the movement for equality between men and women, has inspired many new theoretical advances and methods of analysis in the social sciences such as anthropology). These meanings alter depending on a person's social position within society, as well as on the specific cultural and historical context in which they are found. These perspectives are also affected by existing power relationships and hierarchies—such as gender, class, and race—between groups or individuals. For example, if an anthropologist was examining how marriage partners are chosen, women would have dramatically different experiences, pressures, and interpretations than men.

These ideas challenged anthropologists to pay more nuanced attention to the dynamics of power and the variety of social positions within society. They also challenged the idea that anthropologists could claim to be neutral observers of a society. As a result, anthropologists had to start considering how their own social position may affect both their relationships with informants and their analysis of a situation.

Academic Influences

During his first visit to Lesotho, Ferguson read Foucault's book *Discipline and Punish: The Birth of the Prison.*[1] Foucault's ideas about discourse* (a particular form of language used in a given field of intellectual inquiry or social practice) influenced Ferguson and the questions he asked about development projects in Lesotho. Ferguson describes this complex concept as a form of language within a field of knowledge that follows specific rules and prescribes "acceptable statements and utterances."[2] Ferguson says that the way things are described and thought about has real effects in the world because it influences and shapes our actions.[3] For example, a development institution might describe Lesotho as having a pre-modern subsistence-based* economy (that is, an economy that does not produce a surplus of goods), untouched by regional or global capitalism* (the social and economic system in which trade and industry are held in private hands and run for the sake of profit). This description will influence the type of interventions understood as being appropriate for bringing a capitalist transformation to the region.

In *Discipline and Punish*, Foucault analyses the prison system. He argues that prisons fail in their aims to reform criminals and reduce crime, while unintentionally succeeding in producing a category of "delinquents." Prisons, along with other social institutions such as hospitals, social assistance organizations, and orphanages operate alongside a discourse about "delinquents" as a "carceral apparatus" (apparatus related to prisons) or "machine." This tries to establish which behaviors are considered to be "normal" by controlling those labeled as illegal or deviant.

"Delinquents" were categorized as a subclass in society whose activities are understood as being part of their characters, rather than a manifestation of the inequalities experienced by those in lower class positions. Characterizing them in this way allows delinquents to be seen as a "politically or economically less dangerous ... form of illegality," who can be controlled through surveillance and incarceration.[4] Foucault refers to these unintended consequences as "instrument-effects." They have effects that support the status quo, or act as instruments of power and domination.

Ferguson's approach was also shaped by his PhD advisor at Harvard University, the American anthropologist Sally Falk Moore.* Moore argues that rules are made and transformed through action, rather than being a stable system that people either conform to or not. Ferguson applies this insight in *The Anti-Politics Machine* to rules about livestock in Lesotho.

NOTES

1   Michel Foucault, *Discipline and Punish: The Birth of the Prison* (Harmondsworth: Penguin, 1979).

2   James Ferguson, *The Anti-Politics Machine: "Development," Depoliticization, and Bureaucratic Power in Lesotho* (Minneapolis, MN: University of Minnesota Press, 1994), 18.

3   Ferguson, *The Anti-Politics Machine*, 18, xiv–xv.

4   Foucault, *Discipline and Punish*, 276–7.

MODULE 3
THE PROBLEM

KEY POINTS

- Development anthropologists* (those studying human behavior and thought as it relates to the field of international development)* believed that the failures of development projects to reduce poverty needed to be analyzed. That would mean those failures could be avoided in the future.

- Neo-Marxists*— those inspired by the work of the political philosopher and economist Karl Marx* in their analysis of social, political, and economic systems—argued that the true objective of development initiatives is to allow wealthy countries to continue exploiting the natural resources of "developing" countries. That is why they fail to reduce poverty.

- Rather than asking why development projects fail, Ferguson asks, "What is it that these projects are in fact doing?"

Core Question

The Anti-Politics Machine: "Development," Depoliticization, and Bureaucratic Power in Lesotho, is a book written by the anthropologist James Ferguson. It looks at the impact of a development project in the Thaba-Tseka region of the southern African nation of Lesotho.* Most people see international development as inherently positive, both as an idea and as a set of institutions and practices, with the aim of alleviating poverty and suffering worldwide. The US President Harry Truman* said in 1949: "For the first time in history humanity possess the knowledge and the skill to relieve the suffering of [those impoverished]."[2] Yet, by the 1980s, it was clear that development

> **❝** It began with my dissatisfaction with the very
> repetitive policy-focused discussions going on at
> the time (in the academy and outside it) concerning
> 'development failure.' The question was always, 'Why
> do development projects fail?' and 'How can we do it
> better the next time?' But these did not seem to me
> very productive questions. Lesotho was knee-deep in
> 'failed' development projects, and to come in and say
> that they were failing seemed to me to be not actually
> saying very much—that was obvious on its face. **❞**
>
> James Ferguson, "Interview with James Ferguson," *Humanity Journal*

projects were failing to achieve social and economic growth, despite
having enormous amounts of monetary, technical, and intellectual
resources invested in them.

Development practitioners seeking better strategies for
implementing projects, and academics developing critical approaches
towards development processes and institutions, were asking one core
question: "Why are these projects not successful?"

James Ferguson took a different approach. Rather than asking why
development projects fail, Ferguson asked: "What is it that these
projects are in fact doing?"[3] Ferguson was asking how development
works "in practice, and what are its effects?"[4] When the book was
written, these questions had been largely overlooked by anthropologists
studying development interventions (with a few exceptions in the
tradition of political economy:* the study of economics at the level of
larger political bodies, such as the nation). But Ferguson's question was
especially pertinent given that, despite the overwhelming failure of
development projects, similar projects were continually being
reimplemented.

The Participants

Since the late 1960s, two different approaches had been taken towards explaining and understanding international development initiatives.[5]

First, academics in the social sciences like the South African anthropologist David Brokensha* and the Scottish American anthropologist A. F. Robertson,*[6] saw their role as providing regional and technical expertise that could be utilized by development practitioners. When development projects failed, these academics did not see this as a fundamental challenge to the aims and intents of development organizations or programs. Instead, they believed that these failures needed to be analyzed in order to avoid failures in the future. Anthropologists worked as critically engaged academics (anthropologists of development). They also worked as practitioners (development anthropologists), employed by development agencies for their expertise and insights about the target population. Development anthropologists believed that an anthropological understanding of a society would allow development agencies to set achievable goals and implement projects successfully.[7] These anthropological insights would be especially valuable as many failures could be attributed to poor planning and implementation. This idea challenged the not-uncommon argument that development failed because of the deficiencies of the societies being targeted.

Second, academics like the Guyanese historian Walter Rodney* and the German American social scientist Andre Gunder Frank* critiqued international development from a neo-Marxist, world-systems and dependency* theoretical perspective. According to this perspective, development initiatives were failing to reduce poverty because this stated objective was not their real objective.[8] The real purpose of development projects, they would argue, is to continue the exploitation of "developing" countries' resources established by means of colonialism* (in the sense of exploitation by foreign states). This process keeps "developing" countries in a state of dependency and underdevelopment.

The Contemporary Debate

Ferguson rejected the idea that development should be seen as either a worthy, but flawed, endeavor, or as a problematic institution that promotes new forms of regional and global domination. Instead, he built on an emerging approach to international development. Political economy theorists, like the South African academic Gavin Williams,* had started to look at development interventions "not for what they don't do or might do, but for what they do."[9]

Ferguson, however, rejected one aspect of this type of analysis. The political economists examined the convergence of the political and economic interests of institutions and individuals within specific development projects. These interests could coincide or conflict with one another. Ferguson saw this approach as flawed, since outcomes do not necessarily align with any of the interests that one may have within a development project.[10] Instead, his approach was to study the development projects' actual effects.

Following the French historian and social theorist Michel Foucault,* Ferguson questioned the way in which development knowledge and practice was based on a specific, culturally and historically mediated, interpretation of reality. The Colombian American anthropologist Arturo Escobar* asked a similar question in his 1984 article, "Discourse and Power in Development: Michel Foucault and the Relevance of his Work to the Third World."[11] Although Ferguson does not cite Escobar, this text, together with *The Anti-Politics Machine*, gave rise to a set of postdevelopment* literature. This literature rejects development as an ethical solution to poverty and inequality. It calls for different strategies—especially political strategies—for fighting poverty and inequality in the "Third World"* (that is, the developing world).

NOTES

1 "*Humanity* Interview with James Ferguson, Pt 1: Development as Swarming State Power," *Humanity Journal*, accessed September 16, 2015, http://humanityjournal.org/blog/humanity-interview-with-james-ferguson-pt-1-development-as-swarming-state-power/; James Ferguson, *The Anti-Politics Machine: "Development," Depoliticization, and Bureaucratic Power in Lesotho* (Minneapolis, MN: University of Minnesota Press, 1994), 13.

2 Arturo Escobar, *Encountering Development: The Making and Unmaking of the Third World* (Princeton: Princeton University Press, 2012), 3.

3 "*Humanity* Interview with James Ferguson, pt 1:" Ferguson, *The Anti-Politics Machine*, 13.

4 Ferguson, *The Anti-Politics Machine*, xɪv.

5 Ferguson, *The Anti-Politics Machine*, 9–21.

6 David Brokensha, et al., eds., *Indigenous Knowledge Systems and Development* (Lanham, MD: University Press of America, 1980); A. F. Robertson, *People and the State: An Anthropology of Planned Development* (Cambridge: Cambridge University Press, 1984).

7 Ferguson, *The Anti-Politics Machine*, 10.

8 Walter Rodney, *How Europe Underdeveloped Africa* (London. Bogle-L'ouverture Publications, 1972); Andre Gunder Frank, *Latin America: Underdevelopment or Revolution* (New York: Monthly Review Press, 1969).

9 Ferguson, *The Anti-Politics Machine*, 13.

10 Ferguson, *The Anti-Politics Machine*, 14.

11 Arturo Escobar, "Discourse and Power in Development: Michel Foucault and the Relevance of his Work to the Third World," *Alternatives* 10, no. 3 (1984): 377–400.

MODULE 4
THE AUTHOR'S CONTRIBUTION

KEY POINTS

- Ferguson argues that the concept of "development"* leads us to view global poverty and powerlessness as symptoms of being "less developed."

- *The Anti-Politics Machine* represented a shift away from the ideological positioning of development as either a benevolent process or as inherently damaging to those targeted by its programs.

- Ferguson addresses what development interventions actually do when they are implemented.

Author's Aims

In *The Anti-Politics Machine: "Development," Depoliticization, and Bureaucratic Power in Lesotho*, James Ferguson argues that the concept and practice of "development" has an unintended consequence. It serves as "a dominant problematic or interpretive grid" through which we understand global poverty and powerlessness. Hunger, poverty, and inadequate health care are seen as symptoms of a country being "less developed" than wealthier nations and therefore in need of development assistance.[2] This concept of development is also imbued with the moral value of "goodness." This, in turn, makes it difficult to question the character and effects of development. Sidestepping the ideological question about why and how the concept of development takes on these characteristics, Ferguson examines how development works in practice and with what effects. He focuses on development interventions in Lesotho* between 1975 and 1984.

> ❝ Like goodness itself, development in our time is a value so firmly entrenched that it seems almost impossible to question it or to refer it to any standard beyond its own. ❞
>
> James Ferguson, *The Anti-Politics Machine: "Development," Depoliticization, and Bureaucratic Power in Lesotho*

There are five parts to Ferguson's book:

- Part 1 provides background information about development interventions in the African nation of Lesotho and discusses the relevant literature.
- The second section analyzes the development discourse*—a term Ferguson uses to refer to the particular language and unspoken assumptions of the discussion used by those engaged in development—about Lesotho. Ferguson shows that this discourse portrays Lesotho in a highly distorted way in order to demonstrate that the development intervention proposed is the appropriate solution to Lesotho's poverty.
- In part 3 Ferguson examines his fieldwork data about the social, economic, and political context of rural Lesotho. Unlike the development discourse, this material emphasizes how the country's economic practices and conditions have been impacted by historical and contemporary regional inequalities.
- Part 4 describes a "rural development" project in Lesotho funded by two Western agencies intended to improve agricultural production and increase the quality of Lesotho's livestock. Ferguson argues this project failed because the development discourse failed to recognize the social and economic realities of life in Lesotho.
- Part 5 discusses why these development projects continue to be implemented by identifying their unintended effects.

This structure takes the reader through the various phases of development: planning, institutional set-up, setting, implementation, and outcomes.

Approach

In the book, Ferguson studies a multi-million dollar development project funded by the World Bank* (an institution based in Washington that gives loans to developing nations in return for reforms in economic policy) and the Canadian International Development Agency (CIDA),* an institution that distributes aid to "developing" nations. The project aimed to improve agricultural production and increase commercial livestock ventures by providing better infrastructure, agricultural inputs like fertilizers and seeds, and more rangeland and veterinarian care for livestock. To find out how this was going to work, and to ascertain its effects, Ferguson conducted 15 months of fieldwork in the highland town of Thaba-Tseka and the nearby village of Mashai.

Throughout his fieldwork, Ferguson used the anthropological method of participant observation.* With this method, researchers develop relationships with informants (people asked to relate their experience) by participating in and observing peoples' daily lives and carrying out structured and semi-structured interviews. By immersing themselves within a particular social and cultural context, researchers gain a better sense of everyday life and the power dynamics within a community than by using interviews alone. Ferguson interacted both with the Canadian development workers implementing the project and with the local people targeted by the intervention.

Using participant observation allowed Ferguson to document the realities of life in Lesotho. He was also able to explore the way this differed from the assumptions made in the planning stage of the project and the assumptions made by the development workers themselves. As a result, Ferguson was able to identify the way in which the development industry produces its discourse about Lesotho and about poverty in the country. Using a Foucauldian* style of analysis (following the work of the influential French social philosopher and historian Michel Foucault),* Ferguson's work also uncovered the "instrument-effects" of this development project—the various side-consequences of following development policy.

Contribution in Context

When *The Anti-Politics Machine* was published in 1990, it represented a substantial shift in the way international development was viewed. Ferguson did not argue that development was a benevolent and worthy process. Neither did he present it as inherently imperialistic (that is, furthering the interests of European nations abroad) and damaging to those targeted by its programs. Rather than assessing whether development is good or bad, Ferguson's originality lay in using Michel Foucault's insights to determine what development projects were actually doing.

Ferguson was one of the first people to employ Foucault's ideas in the study of international development and to combine them with anthropological fieldwork techniques. Ferguson took up Foucault's idea of discourse and his analysis of the prison system. In *The Anti-Politics Machine*, he argues that development agencies produce a specific discourse about poorer countries that portrays them as lacking in development. This portrayal proscribes the type of interventions that are implemented, regardless of the actual economic, social, and political circumstances. Ferguson also shows that development projects have effects that were not originally intended by their planners.[3]

Following Foucault's idea of "instrument-effects," these effects serve as a way to exercise power.

NOTES

1   James Ferguson, *The Anti-Politics Machine: "Development," Depoliticization, and Bureaucratic Power in Lesotho* (Minneapolis, MN: University of Minnesota Press, 1994), XIII.

2   Ferguson, *The Anti-Politics Machine*, XIII

3   Michel Foucault, *Discipline and Punish: The Birth of the Prison* (Harmondsworth: Penguin, 1979), 276–7.

SECTION 2
IDEAS

MAIN IDEAS

KEY POINTS

- Ferguson examines the relationship between the "intentionality of planning" in development* projects and development's unintended outcomes and effects.

- He argues that development acts as an "anti-politics machine" by denying the importance of politics as a factor in the experience and existence of poverty.

- *The Anti-Politics Machine* is intended for an academic audience.

Key Themes

In *The Anti-Politics Machine: "Development," Depoliticization, and Bureaucratic Power in Lesotho,* James Ferguson investigates the concept and practice of "development." He bases his arguments on his anthropological* research of a specific development intervention in Lesotho.* This intervention ran from 1975 to 1984. One major theme characterizes Ferguson's analysis: an exploration of the relationship between the "intentionality of planning" in development projects and the unintended outcomes and effects of these projects.[2] Ferguson uses a Foucauldian* framework to explain this relationship. Michel Foucault* describes the interplay between institutions and discourses* as operating like a "machine."[3] Ferguson uses this idea to argue that the "conceptual apparatus" of the international development "machine" includes the particular kind of knowledge that is generated by development agencies about poor countries. This "knowledge" leads to particular strategies being viewed as appropriate to solve poverty within these countries. This, in turn, shapes how the development project is implemented through the "institutional apparatus."[4]

> ❝ In this perspective, the 'development' apparatus in Lesotho is not a machine for eliminating poverty that is incidentally involved with state bureaucracy; it is a machine for reinforcing and expanding the exercise of bureaucratic state power, which incidentally takes 'poverty' as its point of entry—launching an intervention that may have no effect on the poverty but does in fact have other concrete effects. ❞
>
> James Ferguson, *The Anti-Politics Machine: "Development," Depoliticization, and Bureaucratic Power in Lesotho*

The work carried out by the development "machine" results in two "instrument-effects": unplanned effects that become instrumental in supporting existing power structures.[5] The first of these is "depoliticization,"* which occurs at a conceptual level (that is, at the level of understanding and discussion concerning development). Ferguson argues that the development discourse about Lesotho denies both the political dimensions of poverty and that political action may help to solve it. In other words, when development knowledge was generated about Lesotho, the political context was not considered as an important factor. Despite this, the second institutional effect of the development project was the extension of state power and control. This occurred through the establishment of government services and oversight in the Thaba-Tseka region.[6]

Exploring the Ideas

Development projects may lead to outcomes that were not intended.[7] To explain this, Ferguson dissects a report on Lesotho[8] made by the World Bank.* For Ferguson this report serves as a window into the "interpretative grid" of development, through which social reality is understood and represented. The report portrays Lesotho as a "less developed country," with a "national economy" based on subsistence agriculture* (that is, an economy that does not produce any agricultural surplus that might be sold for profit).

Lesotho's isolation and lack of capitalist* trade—trade for private profit being one of the defining features of the economic and social system of capitalism—are seen as the root causes of poor living standards. In the report, Lesotho's economy is also seen as reacting to policies set by the national government, a principle that Ferguson refers to as "governmentality."*[9] By this he means the assumption made by development discourse that a national economy is "almost perfectly responsive to national government policy."[10] Lesotho is a "less developed country" because government action has not provided the resources or guidance to transform the economy into one based on capitalist trade.

Ferguson shows that this report seriously distorts reality. Instead of a national economy based on subsistence agriculture, Lesotho imports a substantial amount of its food from neighboring South Africa. In addition, most of the male labor force migrates to South Africa to work in the mining industries.[11] But, Ferguson argues that the report is not the result of poor scholarship. Instead, the authors aim to position Lesotho as a "promising candidate" for a model of intervention that could be applied to a variety of situations. This model provides technological improvements for agriculture and animal farming. The aim is to ensure that this is seen as the best solution to Lesotho's poverty.

The development project in Thaba-Tseka did not meet its stated objectives of improving commercial agriculture and livestock production. But it did have two unintended consequences.[12] By bringing government services and oversight to the Thaba-Tseka region, the "bureaucratic power" of the state was significantly expanded. The Thaba-Tseka region had been a stronghold for the opposition to the Basotho National Party's* authoritarian* regime, so in effect Thaba-Tseka was brought under the control of the state.

Ferguson argues that this was neither intended nor based on any alliance between the government and development agencies. It came about because the core aim of the project was to improve infrastructure and government services.[13] But by viewing the state as a politically neutral entity concerned with the well-being of its citizens, ongoing political struggles for power were obscured. [14]

The second unintended outcome occurs within the conceptual framework of development agencies. Since poverty is understood as having technical solutions, such as infrastructure, the political dimensions of poverty are overlooked. In Ferguson's words, development is "depoliticized"[15] even though the state is also in effect extended.

Language and Expression

Throughout *The Anti-Politics Machine*, Ferguson borrows terminology associated with Foucault, such as "discourse" (for Ferguson, this means a codified form of language used in a given field of intellectual inquiry or social practice) and "instrument-effect"* (the unintended effects of following a particular course of action). While this terminology can be difficult to understand, Ferguson takes his time to explain and rephrase his assertions in a highly accessible manner: "As Foucault has shown, discourse is a practice, it is structured, and it has real effects which are much more profound than simply 'mystification.' The thoughts and actions of 'development' bureaucrats are powerfully shaped by the world of acceptable statements and utterances within which they live; and what they do and do not do is a product not only of the interests of various nations, classes, or international agencies, but also and at the same time, of a working out of this complex structure of knowledge."[16] That said, Ferguson's book is intended for an academic audience. It is aimed at those working within anthropology* and studying development institutions and interventions.

Although Ferguson did not coin the term "anti-politics," his book has contributed substantially to the increasing use of this term within academic literature about development. Those who talk about the "anti-politics machine" are highlighting Ferguson's insights about the tendency to "depoliticize" the analysis of poverty in discussions about development. They are also referring to the unintended consequences of development, such as promoting and extending state power over people's lives.[17]

NOTES

1   James Ferguson, *The Anti-Politics Machine: "Development," Depoliticization, and Bureaucratic Power in Lesotho* (Minneapolis, MN: University of Minnesota Press, 1994), xiii; 20–1.

2   Ferguson, *The Anti-Politics Machine*, xiii, 20–1.

3   Ferguson, *The Anti-Politics Machine*, xv, original emphasis.

4   Ferguson, *The Anti-Politics Machine*, xiv–xv.

5   Ferguson, *The Anti-Politics Machine*, 255.

6   Ferguson, *The Anti-Politics Machine*, 65, 256

7   Ferguson, *The Anti-Politics Machine*, 20–1.

8   World Bank, *Lesotho: A Development Challenge* (Washington, DC: World Bank, 1975).

9   Ferguson, *The Anti-Politics Machine*, 64.

10 Ferguson, *The Anti-Politics Machine*, 64.

11 For example, Colin Murray, *Families Divided: The Impact of Migrant Labour in Lesotho* (New York: Cambridge University Press, 1981).

12 Ferguson, *The Anti-Politics Machine*, 255–6.

13 Ferguson, *The Anti-Politics Machine*, 195.

14 Ferguson, *The Anti-Politics Machine*, 65.

15 Ferguson, *The Anti-Politics Machine*, 256.

16 Ferguson, *The Anti-Politics Machine*, 18.

17 For example, see Pieter de Vries, "Don't Compromise Your Desire for Development! A Lacanian/Deleuzian Rethinking of the Anti-Politics Machine," *Third World Quarterly* 28, no. 1 (2007): 25–43; Bram Büscher, "Anti-Politics as Political Strategy: Neoliberalism and Transfrontier Conservation in Southern Africa," *Development and Change* 41, no. 1 (2010): 29–51.

SECONDARY IDEAS

KEY POINTS

- The secondary ideas developed by James Ferguson relate to the in-depth data he gathered about the specific social, economic, and political contexts of Lesotho.*

- These ideas support Ferguson's arguments by providing the evidence for his main argument.

- One way Ferguson shows that the developmental representation of Lesotho is inaccurate is by examining the significance of cattle to the local Basotho* population.

Other Ideas

In *The Anti-Politics Machine: "Development," Depoliticization, and Bureaucratic Power in Lesotho,* James Ferguson analyzes a World Bank* and CIDA (Canadian International Development Agency)* funded development* project in the Thaba–Tseka region of Lesotho. Ferguson spent 15 months carrying out fieldwork in this region, examining the social, economic, and political realities of Lesotho. His work helps to show the country's relationship to regional, and global, political and economic structures.

Before the development project was launched, a report about Lesotho was produced for the World Bank, portraying Lesotho as a subsistence agriculture* economy, isolated, and "producing under primitive, ancient techniques."[1] In fact, Ferguson argues, Lesotho has been intensely connected to, and transformed by, regional political and economic structures since at least the mid-nineteenth century. At the time of the Thaba-Tseka project, about half the adult male population was laboring abroad in the South African mining industry.[2] Estimates

> ❝ 'The Bovine Mystique': this book has an excellent
> central chapter with a captivating title. Ferguson
> explains how the enthusiasm of the Basotho for
> accumulating cattle is not, as foreign observers have
> tended to suppose, irrational traditionalism, but vital
> political-economic practice. ❞
>
> A. F. Robertson, Review of *The Anti-Politics Machine*

show that 70 percent of the average household income in the project area was from wage labor in South Africa, with only 6 percent from farming.[3] As only 10 percent of the land within Lesotho is arable, this low reliance on agriculture is not surprising.[4] But it is surprising that the development discourse* about Lesotho portrays it as a subsistence agricultural economy.

Ferguson's work also reveals the significance of cattle both to the local people and in the local economy. A major goal of the World Bank/CIDA development project in Thaba-Tseka was to increase cattle production and improve animal farming techniques and the quality of rangeland. But the Basotho people (the ethnic group that makes up most of the population of Lesotho) were not interested in selling their cattle. Like colonial* officials—those administering the African interests of European nations—had done before them, development planners interpreted this as symptomatic of Basotho "traditional" values. These values were seen as one of the last barriers in transforming the local subsistence economy into a market-based economy. But Ferguson opposes this view. He shows that the Basotho attitude towards cattle is related to labor migration to South Africa. It is not simply an irrational adherence to "tradition."

Exploring the Ideas

The Basotho men accumulate cattle as a "special sort of 'retirement fund.'" Cash can be used to buy cattle, but cattle can only be sold for cash if an individual has no other way to obtain money.[5] Investing money into cattle therefore provides a safety net in case a man loses his job or becomes too ill to continue working. As a "retirement fund," it is effective because it is not easily accessible.[6]

Cattle also fulfill another social function. They represent an exclusively male form of property, over which women have no say. Men are highly motivated to maintain the cultural norm that allows them to convert cash into a form of property that is not accessible to anyone else.[7] But this makes cattle a highly contested arena between men and women, as women may be in need of the money that their migrant husband can provide.

One of the goals of the World Bank/CIDA development project was to reduce the number of cattle in Thaba-Tseka. Doing so would lessen the environmental impact of the animals. The aim was to exchange the large quantities of cattle with fewer, but better breeds. These animals could then be sold in a capitalist* market. But the Basotho people were reluctant to take on these changes. Ferguson argues that this has little to do with "traditional values" standing in the way of economically rational production. For him, this ignores the true value of cattle for the Basotho, especially in the context of labor migration. The Basotho men continuously recreate and reinvest in cattle as a way to ensure their long-term economic stability. They use cattle to secure economic stability outside the claims of the women in their households.

Overlooked

Ferguson argues that while there is a depoliticization* of poverty (a denial of the political causes of and solutions to poverty) within development discourse, development projects tend to result in the expansion of state power. This is often unintentional. Ferguson repeatedly claims that it "goes on behind the backs" of development planners and workers; their intention in implementing the development project does not necessarily have political goals in mind.[8] But he argues that the result is that development becomes a "preeminently political operation."[9] This argument is often overlooked.

Yet, as Ferguson argues, the political benefits of development to those in power does help to explain one mystery: "It does become less mysterious why 'failed' development projects should end up being replicated again and again. It is perhaps reasonable to suggest that it may even be because development projects turn out to have such uses, even if they are in some sense unforeseen, that they continue to attract so much interest and support."[10]

Part of the reason that this has been overlooked is because it seems contradictory to say that projects are replicated because they unwittingly support the expansion of state power. The Canadian anthropologist Tania Murray Li,* for example, rejects the idea that the expansion of the state was an unintended effect of development in Lesotho. She argues that development planners explicitly set out to bring government services and infrastructure to the Thaba-Tseka region.[11] Meanwhile, the Dutch sociologist Bram Büscher* argues against focusing on the expansion of state power. He says that this fails to capture Ferguson's key point in full: that depoliticization is also a political strategy. Using his own data on transfrontier conservation policies in southern Africa, Büscher shows that depoliticization privileges the interests of some organizations at the expense of those who may contest them. This is particularly the case in the context of neoliberal* conservation (environmental protection) strategies. Typical of the economic and political positions of neoliberal principles, these strategies seek to turn conservation into a privatized commodity, positioning it in a market economy outside government control or regulation.[12]

NOTES

1   James Ferguson, *The Anti-Politics Machine: "Development," Depoliticization, and Bureaucratic Power in Lesotho* (Minneapolis, MN: University of Minnesota Press, 1994), 66.

2   Ferguson, *The Anti-Politics Machine*, 112.

3   Ferguson, *The Anti-Politics Machine*, 112.

4   Ferguson, *The Anti-Politics Machine*, 3.

5   Ferguson, *The Anti-Politics Machine*, 158.

6   Ferguson, *The Anti-Politics Machine*, 158.

7   Ferguson, *The Anti-Politics Machine*, 151.

8   Ferguson, *The Anti-Politics Machine*,18

9   Ferguson, *The Anti-Politics Machine*, xv.

10 Ferguson, *The Anti-Politics Machine*, 256.

11 Tania Murray Li, "Compromising Power: Development, culture, and rule in Indonesia," *Cultural Anthropology* 14, no. 3 (1999).

12 Bram Büscher, "Anti-Politics as Political Strategy: Neoliberalism and Transfrontier Conservation in Southern Africa," *Development and Change* 41, no. 1 (2010): 33.

ACHIEVEMENT

KEY POINTS

- Ferguson's most significant achievement was to use the French philosopher Michel Foucault's* ideas about discourse* to guide his analysis of development* in Lesotho.*

- Ferguson uses detailed evidence gathered during his long-term fieldwork to support his overarching arguments about the unintended effects of development interventions.

- *The Anti-Politics Machine* is based on Ferguson's analysis of a development project in one country. That limits the extent to which his findings can be generalized.

Assessing the Argument

In *The Anti-Politics Machine: "Development," Depoliticization, and Bureaucratic Power in Lesotho*, James Ferguson encourages readers to consider a new question. Previous commentators had focused either on why development initiatives fail, or on whether development endeavors are inherently benevolent or not. In contrast, Ferguson asks, "What do development projects do?" and "Why do these projects continue to be implemented despite continually failing to meet their short-term and long-term objectives?" To explore these questions Ferguson employs the theoretical framework about discourse proposed by the French thinker Michel Foucault. He explores how the language and knowledge used in development creates its own reality and rationales.

Ferguson's overarching argument is that development interventions have unintended effects. Specifically, they have the effect of denying

> ❝ Ferguson's *The Anti-Politics Machine* is a rigorous and largely successful attempt to extend Foucault's cultural analysis into new domains. It reminds us that the terrains of representation and institutional practices are important social and political arenas of struggle. They are crucial for reimagining the 'Third World.' ❞
>
> Arturo Escobar, "Review of *The Anti-Politics Machine*"

that there are political causes of poverty while simultaneously leading to the expansion of state control. He supports this argument with detailed evidence gathered during his long-term fieldwork in Lesotho between 1982 and 1983. By using the anthropological* method of participant observation,* Ferguson was able to join in with and observe peoples' daily lives. In doing so, he captured the power-dynamics at play in the community. This ethnographic* material—material accumulated by the systematic study of people—allowed Ferguson to explore the social and political realities of life in Lesotho. In his book, he successfully places this alongside the less-nuanced way in which development planners and workers were describing the country and its problems.

Achievement in Context

The Anti-Politics Machine is widely recognized and cited in development studies and, in particular, in the anthropological study of development. Its success when it was first published was partly due to Ferguson's use of the theories of Michel Foucault. Foucault had gained substantial influence in the social sciences, including anthropology,* since the 1970s. He investigated the ways in which knowledge is shaped by existing power structures and can legitimize or marginalize certain groups. While knowledge may be considered an objective and scientifically neutral area, it is, in reality, a battlefield, constructed by dominant social and historical forces.

Ferguson applied these Foucauldian* ideas to international development organizations and projects. His approach influenced a new wave of postdevelopment* academics, a group that grew in prominence during the 1990s. Postdevelopment academics study the ways that development knowledge and practice comes into being, and question its purpose. They argue that development is not an ethical solution to poverty and inequality and that alternative strategies should be developed. *The Anti-Politics Machine* is widely recognized as one of the early examples of this type of questioning and analysis. It stands alongside *Encountering Development: The Making and Unmaking of the Third World* (1995) by the Columbian American anthropologist Arturo Escobar.[1]

Limitations

The Anti-Politics Machine is an intensive analysis of a large-scale development project. Ferguson's analysis focuses on a specific place and time period: the mountainous Thaba-Tseka region of Lesotho between 1975 and 1984. As with most anthropological research, the specific historical and social setting of this work makes it difficult to apply Ferguson's findings to other contexts. Anticipating this, Ferguson tries to draw comparisons. He highlights similarities between the project in Lesotho and those in other African contexts, such as South Africa, Tanzania, and Zimbabwe.[2] He also argues that development discourse is generally very similar regardless of the specific context in which a project is implemented. That is because development discourse emphasizes technical change, with development personnel tending to be experts in technical implementation, rather than experts on the social, political, or economic context of their projects.[3]

But Lesotho also has unique features. The country is very dependent on South Africa. Estimates from the late 1970s show that about half the adult male population took work as migrant laborers in the South African mining industry.[4] As a result, Lesotho has little control over its economic success or future.[5] Ferguson claims that this situation allows for the paradoxical state of depoliticization* and the simultaneous extension of state power to reveal itself in a more obvious way in Lesotho. This claim suggests that if depoliticization and extension of state control are not found in other contexts, then it is because they are less apparent in these contexts, not that they do not occur. This may be the case, even if Ferguson's evidence, in itself, does not prove it. Regardless, it is an analysis that has encouraged other anthropologists to examine whether these processes can be found in other contexts; their findings have supported Ferguson's argument about depoliticization.

The Anti-Politics Machine has also been influential in the interdisciplinary context of development studies (a field that, being interdisciplinary, is of interest to researchers who specialize in different aspects of the social sciences and economics). Here, non-anthropologists are examining more critically the type of language and knowledge used by development institutions. But this has not significantly transformed development policy or discourse. As Ferguson argues, development knowledge is not the product of poor scholarship used by development institutions. Rather, it has the more systematic purpose of justifying the type of interventions that development organizations specialize in.

NOTES

1   Arturo Escobar, *Encountering Development: The Making and Unmaking of the Third World* (Princeton: Princeton University Press, 2012).

2   James Ferguson, *The Anti-Politics Machine: "Development," Depoliticization, and Bureaucratic Power in Lesotho* (Minneapolis, MN: University of Minnesota Press, 1994), 257–67.

3   Ferguson, *The Anti-Politics Machine*, 258–9.

4   Ferguson, *The Anti-Politics Machine*, 112.

5   Ferguson, *The Anti-Politics Machine*, 257.

MODULE 8
PLACE IN THE AUTHOR'S WORK

KEY POINTS

- James Ferguson explores the topics of poverty, inequality, and social change in southern Africa. He also looks at these in the context of global political and economic forces.

- *The Anti-Politics Machine*, published in 1990, was James Ferguson's first book. It was based on his 1985 PhD thesis.

- Although Ferguson has written three books since *The Anti-Politics Machine*, it remains his best-known and most influential book.

Positioning

The Anti-Politics Machine: "Development," Depoliticization, and Bureaucratic Power in Lesotho was James Ferguson's first book. Based on his 1985 PhD thesis, the book was published in 1990. While Ferguson has written a further three books, *The Anti-Politics Machine* remains his best-known work. Its innovative critique of development* means it is widely cited both by anthropologists studying development and within development studies itself. Since the book was published, academics have regularly taken *The Anti-Politics Machine* as a point of departure for their own work. This has led to critically thought-out challenges to Ferguson's theoretical framework and conclusions.[1] Ferguson has not, however, modified his arguments or conclusions developed in *The Anti-Politics Machine*.[2]

Although, after the publication of *The Anti-Politics Machine*, Ferguson moved away from the examination of development institutions and interventions, he has remained interested in the

> **"** I should say I've not worked on these questions of development projects for many, many years ... I am, however, skeptical that things are terribly different from the way they were when I first started working on these issues ... the development industry has trotted out new languages and new justifications to explain that now things are going to be done fundamentally differently. I can tell you that is what was being said in the late 1970s too, when they were doing all these 'integrated rural development' projects all over Africa. **"**
>
> James Ferguson, "James Ferguson on Modernity, Development, and Reading Foucault in Lesotho," *Theory Talks*

relationship between development and anthropology.* In an essay of 1997, he argues that development shares many conceptual assumptions with anthropology. Development is thus anthropology's "evil twin."[3] The difference between the two is that anthropology has thoroughly unpacked most of those conceptual assumptions. During the 1980s anthropologists debated how an individual's social position is embedded in a web of power relations—the interplay of different levels of social and political status and authority. At the same time, anthropologists also started to question their position in relation to those they studied. They debated the established claim that anthropology can produce objective knowledge about a culture. The conclusion was that anthropology could serve as another way in which power is exercised over a culture. This understanding prompted anthropologists to be more aware and questioning of their own conceptual frameworks.

Integration

In his later works Ferguson moved away from examining development interventions in the way that he did in *The Anti-Politics*

Machine. But he did continue to explore the issues of poverty, inequality, and social change in southern Africa in the context of global political and economic forces. His second book, *Expectations of Modernity: Myths and Meanings of Urban Life on the Zambian Copperbelt* (1999), examines what modernity means in a copper-mining town in Zambia. Zambia's once profitable copper industry fell into sharp decline in the mid-1970s, upsetting expectations of continuing progress and prosperity.[4] In his book *Global Shadows: Africa in the Neo-Liberal World Order* (2006),[5] Ferguson went on to explore the implications and effects of the neoliberal* economic policies that began to be imposed on African states by international financial institutions in the 1990s. These policies emphasize privatization and deregulation of industry.

In a number of papers and coedited books, Ferguson has gone on to develop a theme he first touched on in *The Anti-Politics Machine*. This addresses the vision of Lesotho as a political entity with a specific territory. Ferguson questions an embedded assumption in anthropology: the idea that space is naturally divided into places with clear boundaries and, further, that cultures and nations are uncritically defined in relation to "place."[6] Along with a coauthor, the Indian American anthropologist Akhil Gupta,* Ferguson explains this. He says it is "so taken for granted that each country embodies its own distinctive culture and society that the terms 'society' and 'culture' are routinely simply appended to the names of nation-states, as when a tourist visits India to understand 'Indian culture' and 'Indian society,' or Thailand to experience 'Thai culture,' or the United States to get a whiff of 'American culture.'"[7] But does culture map onto spaces as easily as we assume?

Significance

While all Ferguson's books have been influential in anthropological studies of development and Africa, none have been as prominent outside anthropology as *The Anti-Politics Machine*. Since the book was published in 1990, Ferguson has delivered over 90 invited lectures to audiences associated with anthropology, interdisciplinary development studies, and interdisciplinary African studies. These lectures have taken place throughout the United States, the United Kingdom, South Africa, Canada, Brazil, Australia, South Korea, China, Japan, Norway, Sweden, the Netherlands, and Belgium. Ferguson was also invited to give an extended interview with Theory Talks, a forum for scholars and students in international relations, in 2009.[8]

As Ferguson's first major publication, *The Anti-Politics Machine* established his reputation for providing critical and insightful examinations of poverty, inequality, and social change in the context of larger regional and global institutions and policies. He is still seen as a leading figure who has shaped ongoing debates about development agencies. And his recent work continues to build on the issues he raised in *The Anti-Politics Machine*. In 2015 Ferguson published *Give a Man a Fish: Reflections on the New Politics of Distribution*.[9] This work challenges the proverb, "Give a man a fish and you feed him for a day; teach a man to fish and you feed him for a lifetime." It looks at the success of the social welfare systems in Africa that distribute cash payments to low-income earners. These programs challenge neoliberal economic assumptions about the alleviation of poverty, founded on the belief that economic growth is best obtained by privatizing economic industries and through government policies that do not interfere in these industries. The success of these programs offers a different view. This book, then, touches on the issue of development—even though Ferguson is not writing about development agencies directly.

NOTES

1 See for example, Tania Murray Li, "Compromising power: Development, Culture, and Rule in Indonesia," *Cultural Anthropology* (1999): 297; Tania Murray Li, *The Will to Improve: Governmentality, Development, and the Practice of Politics* (Durham: Duke University Press, 2007).

2 See "*Humanity* Interview with James Ferguson, pt 1: Development as Swarming State Power," *Humanity Journal*, accessed September 16, 2015, http://humanityjournal.org/blog/humanity-interview-with-james-ferguson-pt-1-development-as-swarming-state-power/; "Theory Talk #34: James Ferguson on Modernity, Development, and Reading Foucault in Lesotho," Theory Talks, accessed September 16, 2015, http://www.theory-talks. org/2009/11/theory-talk-34.html; "Polar Interview with James Ferguson and Akhil Gupta," accessed September 16, 2015, http://www.polaronline. org/2012/04/15/james-ferguson-and-akhil-gupta/.

3 James Ferguson, "Anthropology and Its Evil Twin: 'Development' in the Constitution of a Discipline," in *International Development and the Social Sciences: Essays on the History and Politics of Knowledge*, ed. Frederick Cooper and Randall Packard (Berkeley: University of California Press, 1997), 150–75.

4 James Ferguson, *Expectations of Modernity: Myths and Meanings of Urban Life on the Zambian Copperbelt* (Berkeley: University of California Press, 1999).

5 James Ferguson, *Global Shadows: Africa in the Neoliberal World Order* (Durham and London: Duke University Press, 2006).

6 James Ferguson and Akhil Gupta, eds., *Culture, Power, Place: Explorations in Critical Anthropology* (London: Duke University Press, 1997); James Ferguson and Akhil Gupta, eds., *Anthropological Locations: Boundaries and Grounds of a Field Science* (Berkeley, CA: University of California Press, 1997).

7 Ferguson and Gupta, *Culture, Power, Place*, 34.

8 "Theory Talk #34."

9 James Ferguson, *Give a Man a Fish: Reflections on the New Politics of Distribution* (Durham: Duke University Press, 2015).

SECTION 3
IMPACT

THE FIRST RESPONSES

KEY POINTS

- For critics of *The Anti-Politics Machine*, the book cannot be thought useful because it does not suggest ways of improving intervention techniques in order to address the needs of local communities.

- Ferguson has responded to this criticism by stating that it was not his intention for the book to be used to generate new policies or techniques.

- *The Anti-Politics Machine* has also received criticism for its portrayal of development* workers as ignorant of the effects of development interventions. Ferguson has not directly responded to this.

Criticism

When James Ferguson first published *The Anti-Politics Machine: "Development," Depoliticization, and Bureaucratic Power in Lesotho* it was well received by many anthropologists working on issues surrounding development.[1] Those more closely engaged with development institutions, however, such as academics providing expert advice or technical assistance, critiqued the book for a number of reasons.

Critics closely associated with development institutions, particularly in southern Africa, argued that the book was not useful in improving intervention techniques to address the needs of local communities.[2] Although Ferguson explicitly stated in his book that this was not its purpose, this remains a major shortcoming for development practitioners.[3]

In *The Anti-Politics Machine*, Ferguson dismisses the Scottish American anthropologist Alexander F. Robertson,* author of *People*

> ❝ 'Why would one suppose that critical thinking is only for things that one is opposed to?' For instance, I think it's crucially important that we think critically about the concept of 'human rights.' Does that mean that I'm in favor of torture and dictators? Certainly not. But the concept of human rights requires very careful, critical scrutiny, precisely because it is something around which we are organizing our political energies and where we're focusing our hopes and ambitions for the future. ❞
>
> James Ferguson, "James Ferguson on Modernity, Development, and Reading Foucault in Lesotho," *Theory Talks*

and the State: An Anthropology of Planned Development (1984),[4] as being uncritical in his views about development. This is based on Robertson's idea that development is the best way to address poverty, even though it does not operate perfectly.[5] Robertson, in turn, offers the most critical review of *The Anti-Politics Machine*. He argues that Ferguson portrays development workers as unable to understand local political and social realities since the "development discourse* does the thinking for them."[6] This portrayal, he argues, is the result of Ferguson's own ideological interpretations, in which academics and local populations are uncritically understood as intelligent but undervalued, while development workers and institutions are powerful but "dumb."[7]

The South American sociologist Pieter de Vries* also critiques Ferguson. He queries Ferguson's focus on the "development machine" instead of on the people who actively or passively support development initiatives.[8] This critique emerges from de Vries's actor-oriented* approach toward development (an approach that examines the diverse interests and understandings of various people involved in a development project and how these may come into conflict when planning and implementing a project).

Responses

Ferguson has responded to some of the criticisms that focus on the perceived "usefulness" (or otherwise) of his book for development practitioners.[9] He reiterates his original position—that it was never his intention to proscribe a new guide for action; rather, his aim was to examine what development actually accomplishes.[10] What he has to say on the question of "what can be done?" is covered in the prologue of *The Anti-Politics Machine*, where he expresses doubt that development interventions will ever produce the intended outcome of alleviating poverty, especially as they do not take into account the political dimensions that contribute to poverty. Ferguson suggests that the political struggles waged by poor people are more likely to be successful than development since these struggles may alter the relationships of power that prevent them from improving their situation. Ferguson argues that anthropologists should make their work available to those engaged in these political struggles, instead of providing advice to development institutions on how to improve their projects.[11]

Ferguson has not specifically addressed critiques about his representation and analysis of development workers and his work has shifted away from examining the actions and effects of development institutions. But *The Anti-Politics Machine* continues to be a site for critical dialogue between anthropologists and those in other disciplines who are studying development projects.

Conflict and Consensus

The way Ferguson positions development practitioners as gears within a machine has been criticized. Despite this, most authors agree with Ferguson's argument that development interventions succeed in "depoliticizing"* poverty by conceptually denying the political causes and solutions to it.

However, more elaborate criticism has emerged from an actor-oriented perspective of development. These criticisms challenge Ferguson's argument that the "development machine" works to deliver specific outcomes "behind the backs of or against the wills of even the most powerful actors."[12] The British anthropologist David Mosse* and the French anthropologist Jean-Pierre Olivier de Sardan,* for example, argue that Ferguson's image of the "development machine" treats development as an all-powerful immovable entity. This image does not recognize the differences between development institutions, their philosophies, and their practices.[13] These critics also argue that an analysis of development needs to account for differences between individuals who work on development projects, who have varying understandings, positions, and interests. This needs to be acknowledged in order to move away from an image of development workers as ignorant and unintelligent.[14]

Although Ferguson has not responded to these objections, the Colombian American anthropologist Arturo Escobar* addresses them in the preface to the 2012 reissue of his book *Encountering Development: The Making and Unmaking of the Third World*. Like Ferguson, Escobar was inspired by the work of Michel Foucault* to examine the ideological background of development discourses. Escobar agrees it is important to understand development in all its complexity and variation. But he argues that these criticisms also raise new problems, particularly as the thoughts or actions of individuals may not, in themselves, have an impact on the bigger picture. Escobar says, "nothing that any actor does can ever amount to a significant challenge to what exists or produce a significantly different thought."[15] As this suggests, the debate about how to approach the study of development is ongoing. No one perspective may explain every aspect of development institutions and their programs.

NOTES

1   See for example, Arturo Escobar, "*The Anti-Politics Machine: 'Development,'*
    Depoliticization, and Bureaucratic Power in Lesotho," *American Ethnologist*
    18, no. 3 Representations of Europe: Transforming State, Society, and
    Identity (1991), 618; Frederick Cooper, "*The Anti-Politics Machine:*
    'Development,' Depoliticization, and Bureaucratic Power in Lesotho," *Journal*
    of Southern African Studies 16, no. 4 (1990), 771–4.

2   These are the critiques by Reintsema, Du Rette and Vordzorgbe compiled
    in James Ferguson, *The Anti-Politics Machine: a Panel Review of James*
    Ferguson's Book, with a Rejoinder by the Author (Roma: National University
    of Lesotho, 1992).

3   James Ferguson, *The Anti-Politics Machine: "Development," Depoliticization,*
    and Bureaucratic Power in Lesotho (Minneapolis, MN: University of
    Minnesota Press, 1994), xiv, 279.

4   Alexander F. Robertson, *People and the State: An Anthropology of Planned*
    Development (Cambridge: Cambridge University Press, 1984).

5   Ferguson, *The Anti-Politics Machine*, 10.

6   Alexander F. Robertson, "*The Anti-Politics Machine: 'Development,'*
    Depoliticization, and Bureaucratic Power in Lesotho by James Ferguson,"
    Journal of International Development 4, no. 3 (1992): 337–40.

7   Robertson, *The Anti-Politics Machine*, 337–40.

8   Pieter de Vries, "A Research Journey: On Actors, Concepts and the Text," in
    Battlefields of Knowledge: The Interlocking of Theory and Practice in Social
    Research and Development, ed. Norman Long and Ann Long (London:
    Routledge, 1992), 47–84.

9   These critiques as well as Ferguson's response are compiled in Ferguson,
    The Anti-Politics Machine: a Panel Review.

10 Ferguson, *The Anti-Politics Machine*, xiv, 279.

11 Ferguson, *The Anti-Politics Machine*, 282–6.

12 Ferguson, *The Anti-Politics Machine*, 18.

13 David Mosse, *Cultivating Development: An Ethnography of Aid Policy and*
    Practice (London: Pluto, 2005); Jean-Pierre Olivier De Sardan, *Anthropology*
    and Development: Understanding Contemporary Social Change (London:
    Zed Books, 2005).

14 For a typical statement of this position, see Mosse, *Cultivating*
    Development, 5–11.

15 Arturo Escobar, *Encountering Development: The Making and Unmaking of the Third World* (Princeton: Princeton University Press, 2012), xvi.

THE EVOLVING DEBATE

KEY POINTS

- James Ferguson convinced anthropologists to pay closer attention to how the development* discourse* generates "knowledge."

- Although Ferguson has not written about development interventions since *The Anti-Politics Machine* was published in 1990, his ideas remain influential.

- New studies of development do not abandon Ferguson's ideas, but they inspect them more closely: using different contexts and from different theoretical orientations.

Uses and Problems

James Ferguson's book *The Anti-Politics Machine: "Development," Depoliticization, and Bureaucratic Power in Lesotho* led to new questions being asked about development interventions. His work persuaded anthropologists and others involved in development to critically examine how knowledge is generated and used within development; the book shows how the language and assumptions that constitute the "conversation" surrounding development—the discourse—may produce certain problematic effects when development is put into practice.

The influence his ideas had is apparent from the title of the edited volume *Discourses of Development: Anthropological Perspectives*, published in 1997.[1] Ferguson also inspired a new group: "postdevelopment"* academics. These scholars began dissecting the ideological aspect of development knowledge and reflecting on alternatives to development interventions and programs.

> ❝I am increasingly dissatisfied with work that treats such critique as the end of the project, as if to say that now we have done our job: 'We've exposed this as political, we've revealed that there are relations of power and inequality behind it all, and we've denounced it. Now we know we're in the right and they're in the wrong. Gotcha!' But a lot of times, this simply demonstrates what everyone knows already … What is more interesting is if you treat that as a beginning. OK, so there is a politics going on here, but where is that going?❞
>
> James Ferguson, "Interview with James Ferguson," *Humanity Journal*

Many scholars now view Ferguson's portrayal of the development discourse as too inflexible and all-encompassing. They argue that more attention needs to be directed towards understanding the individual motivations, conceptualizations, and actions of development workers. The South American sociologist Pieter deVries* was the first to highlight this problem in Ferguson's work.[2] Since then, it has been extensively reemphasized by scholars including the British anthropologists Emma Crewe,* Elizabeth Harrison,* and David Mosse.*[3]

New studies critically reexamine Ferguson's ideas; the Canadian anthropologist Tania Murray Li,* for example, has looked at Ferguson's use of the term "governmentality."* Foucault used this term to refer to institutions and methods of governing a group of people that "acts on or through the agencies and subjectivities of individuals."[4] In contrast, Ferguson uses the term to refer to an assumption made by development discourse: the assumption that a national government can control its national economy.[5] Li reexamines this idea and Ferguson's depoliticization* effect in her study of a resettlement program in Indonesia.[6]

Schools of Thought

The Anti-Politics Machine is one of the most cited works in studies that apply anthropological critiques to development. One of the main reasons for the book's influence was Ferguson's application of Michel Foucault's* insights about the nature of knowledge. Although Arturo Escobar* had already applied Foucault's idea of discourse to development, *The Anti-Politics Machine* was the first published book to take this perspective;[7] consequently Ferguson is seen as a leading figure in the postdevelopment school of thought (even if he may not define himself that way). Postdevelopment literature examines the historical context in which development discourse developed and how it can be seen today, an approach exemplified in Escobar's work *Encountering Development: The Making and Unmaking of the Third World*.[8] Those taking this approach towards development express skepticism about the potential of development interventions to alleviate poverty and address inequality. They often call for alternative approaches outside the context of development. These approaches include supporting and documenting the political struggles of those who are marginalized.[9]

Other anthropologists studying development since the late 1990s have examined the premises of Ferguson's work in many institutional contexts and projects. Some, such as the British anthropologist David Mosse, follow Ferguson in adopting a Foucauldian* perspective on the way knowledge is constructed within development. They are, however, more closely aligned with an "actor-oriented" approach, as articulated by British sociologist and anthropologist Norman Long* in 1992.[10] This approach involves a focus on the varying interests, understandings, and practices that exist in development projects. They argue that this is a crucial aspect, since development discourses may be transformed within a context of debate and compromise, and as such, do not necessarily translate into practice.[11] As Norman Long argued, "development intervention models … become strategic weapons in the hands of those charged with promoting them. Yet the battle never ends, since all actors exercise some kind of 'power,' leverage or room for manoeuvre, even those in highly subordinate positions."[12]

In Current Scholarship

Despite the fact that James Ferguson has not written on development interventions since *The Anti-Politics Machine*, his ideas about development remain influential. Authors writing about development interventions continue to use his insights to position their own analyses. But Ferguson's Foucauldian style of analysis has proved less popular. This is partly because of a general trend in scholarship: one that recognizes that using multiple theoretical perspectives can give a better understanding of a specific project.

A recent example of this is seen in the work of Tania Murray Li. In *The Will to Improve: Governmentality, Development, and the Practice of Politics* (2007), Li examines historical and contemporary development interventions in the highlands of Indonesia.[13] She revisits Ferguson's conclusion that one effect of the development discourse is the depoliticization of poverty. Similarly, she argues that in "rendering development as technical," certain techniques are construed as appropriate for intervention. At the same time this suggests that these technical interventions are "nonpolitical."[14] Li analyses the depoliticization effect further by arguing that this process is limited by politics itself, as happens if the process generates political challenges from those targeted by the interventions. In making this argument, Li is following Ferguson in analyzing the structural effects of a development project. But she is also aware of the different interests and understanding of the people involved in the development intervention. In this way she builds on, and enriches, Ferguson's ideas.[15]

NOTES

1   Ralph D. Grillo and Roderick L. Stirrat, eds., *Discourses of Development: Anthropological Perspectives* (Oxford and New York: Berg, 1997).

2   Pieter de Vries, "A Research Journey: On Actors, Concepts and the Text," in *Battlefields of Knowledge: The Interlocking of Theory and Practice in Social Research and Development*, ed. Norman Long and Ann Long (London: Routledge, 1992), 47–84.

3   David Mosse, *Cultivating Development: An Ethnography of Aid Policy and Practice* (London: Pluto, 2005); see also, Jan Nederveen Pieterse, "My Paradigm or Yours? Alternative Development, Post-Development, Reflexive Development," *Development and Change* 29, no. 2 (1998): 363.

4   Michel Foucault, "Governmentality," in *The Foucault Effect: Studies in Governmentality with Two Lectures by and an Interview with Michel Foucault*, ed. Graham Burchell et al. (Chicago: Chicago University Press, 1991),102; Mosse, Cultivating Development, 6.

5   James Ferguson, *The Anti-Politics Machine: "Development," Depoliticization, and Bureaucratic Power in Lesotho* (Minneapolis, MN: University of Minnesota Press, 1994), 64.

6   Tania Murray Li, "Compromising power: Development, Culture, and Rule in Indonesia," *Cultural Anthropology* (1999): 297; Tania Murray Li, *The Will to Improve: Governmentality, Development, and the Practice of Politics* (Durham: Duke University Press, 2007).

7   Arturo Escobar, "Discourse and Power in Development: Michel Foucault and the Relevance of his Work to the Third World," *Alternatives* 10, no. 3 (1984): 377–400.

8   Arturo Escobar, *Encountering Development: The Making and Unmaking of the Third World* (Princeton: Princeton University Press, 2012), xvi.

9   See for instance, Arturo Escobar, "Imagining a post-development era? Critical thought, development and social movements," *Social text* (1992): 20–56.

10 Norman Long and Ann Long, eds, *Battlefields of Knowledge: The Interlocking of Theory and Practice in Social Research and Development* (London: Routledge, 1992), 47–84; see also Alberto Arce and Norman Long, *Anthropology, Development, and Modernities: Exploring Discourses, Counter-tendencies, and Violence* (London and New York: Routledge, 2000).

11 David Mosse, *Cultivating Development: An Ethnography of Aid Policy and Practice* (London: Pluto, 2005), 5–11.

12 Norman Long, *Development Sociology: Actor Perspectives* (London and New York: Routledge, 2003), 17.

13 Murray Li, *The Will to Improve*.

14 Murray Li, The Will to Improve, 7.

15 See also, Mark Schuller, *Killing with Kindness: Haiti, International Aid, and NGOs* (New Brunswick, NJ: Rutgers University Press, 2012).

IMPACT AND INFLUENCE TODAY

KEY POINTS

- *The Anti-Politics Machine* has shaped the way in which anthropologists today approach the study of development.*

- Some development economists have also started to introduce Ferguson's insights about development interventions into their work.

- Ferguson's arguments are often seen as frustrating because they fail to provide concrete ways of addressing poverty.

Position

The Anti-Politics Machine: "Development," Depoliticization, and Bureaucratic Power in Lesotho by James Ferguson was published in 1990 and remains a widely cited text, influential in the fields of the anthropology* of development and development studies. Authors offering a broad picture of the anthropological study of development continue to devote sections to Ferguson. They focus on his call for a more critical look at the kinds of knowledge created by powerful development institutions, which is then used to inform their policies and programs.[1] *The Anti-Politics Machine* is considered a classic because it brought the theoretical insights of Michel Foucault* to bear on international development. This has fundamentally shaped the way in which anthropologists today approach the study of development. Foucault's concept of discourse,* for example, is now used widely. Many authors, among them the Canadian anthropologist Tania Murray Li,* continue to build on Ferguson's insight that

> **66** The alternatives to conventional development are
> seldom clearly spelled out. For some the answer lies in
> people driving development themselves, while others
> emphasise the need for localised strategies determined
> by group participation or appropriate technologies or
> redistributive justice. **99**
>
> Emma Crewe and Richard Axelby, *Anthropology and Development: Culture,
> Morality and Politics in a Globalised World.*

development discourse often has the effect of depoliticizing* the
causes and solutions to poverty worldwide.

The Anti-Politics Machine is not just read by anthropologists. Many
students of anthropology and development studies go on to work in
non-governmental* and bilateral aid* organizations (organizations
that administer the giving of aid from one country to another), or in
development financial institutions like the World Bank.* In addition,
some development economists have used Ferguson's insights to
contribute to ongoing debates within this practical field.

Interaction

Development economists were once seen as approaching development
in a fundamentally different way from anthropologists. But some have
now started to use Ferguson's insights about the way in which
development knowledge is produced in their own work. Mainstream
authors such as the American economist Jeffrey Sachs* continue to
emphasize the role of geography and environmental conditions in
creating and perpetuating poverty. This is used as a way to explain and
promote development interventions:[2] it legitimizes projects that are
created to try to compensate for the geographical limitations that
affect productivity. But those who are critical of this viewpoint use
Ferguson's insights to highlight the political and institutional factors
that also have a profound effect on economic development.

The American economist William Easterly* is one of the most vocal of these critics. He often evokes Ferguson's analysis of development institutions and planners, drawing attention to the problematic and often inadequate understanding of the historical, political, and social context in which projects are being established. However, Easterly also uses Ferguson's arguments to advance his own neoliberal* formula for economic development—a formula that calls for privatization and a minimum of government interference in the economy.[3]

In his later works, Ferguson has developed strong criticisms of the neoliberal economics and policies that are imposed on countries as an essential ingredient for their economic development and success. This is particularly the case in Ferguson's 2006 publication, *Global Shadows: Africa in the Neoliberal World Order*.[4]

The Continuing Debate

The Anti-Politics Machine opened the gates for a new group of scholars known as postdevelopment* theorists. Their work:

- Explores how the assumptions that affect development discourse developed over time
- Calls for alternatives to international development, particularly by supporting the political struggles of marginalized groups.

Postdevelopment theorists are characteristically extremely skeptical about development as a way to address global poverty and inequality. In a similar way to the world-systems and dependency theorists* of the 1970s (according to whom the unequal development of economies can be explained by a capitalist* world order in which the wealthy "core" economies extract resources from the poor "peripheral" economies, keeping them in a state of dependency and underdevelopment), this group typically see development as a powerful global phenomenon that supports existing forms of power and hierarchy.

In many cases, Ferguson is considered to be a leading figure in the emergence of postdevelopment scholarship. Alongside Arturo Escobar* Ferguson provided its theoretical framework. While he would probably not describe himself as a postdevelopment theorist, critiques of his ideas often form part of a wider critique of postdevelopment literature. The most common criticism is leveled against this school's overtly negative view of development. It is also criticized for failing to provide alternative approaches that can lead to planned action. These criticisms are also leveled against *The Anti-Politics Machine.*

Postdevelopment theorists suggest that research about the communities targeted by development interventions should be made available to these communities. This could take the form of local groups who work on behalf of the impoverished and oppressed: labor unions, opposition parties, and Church groups.[5] However, actually putting this into action is problematic; while these groups may advocate against inequality, they often do so at the expense of another group. So, whether or not the theories of postdevelopment are convincing, these arguments provoke frustration. They provide no answer to the question "What can we do, or what should we do, when faced with the realities of extreme inequality and poverty?"[6]

NOTES

1   See for example, Emma Crewe and Richard Axelby, *Anthropology and Development: Culture, Morality and Politics in a Globalised World* (Cambridge, Cambridge University Press, 2012).

2   See for instance, Jeffrey D. Sachs, *The End of Poverty* (New York: Penguin, 2005).

3   See for example, William Easterly, *The White Man's Burden: Why the West's Efforts to Aid the Rest Have Done So Much Ill and So Little Good* (New York: Penguin, 2006), 193–4.

4   James Ferguson, *Global Shadows: Africa in the Neoliberal World Order* (Durham and London: Duke University Press, 2006).

5   James Ferguson, *The Anti-Politics Machine: "Development," Depoliticization, and Bureaucratic Power in Lesotho* (Minneapolis, MN: University of Minnesota Press, 1994), 286–7.

6   See for example, Pieter de Vries, "Don't Compromise Your Desire for Development! A Lacanian/Deleuzian Rethinking of the Anti-Politics Machine," *Third World Quarterly* 28, no. 1 (2007): 25–43.

WHERE NEXT?

KEY POINTS

- Ferguson's ideas continue to influence anthropologists*
  and those involved in development* planning.

- Ferguson's idea that development discourse*
  depoliticizes* the causes of poverty continues to resonate
  with academics today.

- Ferguson has inspired anthropologists to identify
  development discourses and how these affect the
  outcomes of development interventions.

Potential

James Ferguson's *The Anti-Politics Machine: "Development,"
Depoliticization, and Bureaucratic Power in Lesotho* is considered a classic
text. Ferguson's major contribution is to apply Michel Foucault's*
ideas about how knowledge is generated and used to the field of
development. Ferguson looks at how the knowledge gathered by
development workers shapes development intervention, and leads to
particular outcomes. This idea of a development discourse has been
frequently invoked in subsequent studies on development
interventions. In addition, Ferguson's insight that development
discourse depoliticizes the causes of poverty continues to resonate
with scholars.

Most scholars, however, now hold the view that Ferguson's
description of the "development machine" lacks nuance. Ferguson
presents development as an all-powerful and monolithic entity. This
ignores important differences between types of development
institutions, policies, and interventions. *The Anti-Politics Machine* has

> ❝I understand your skepticism about 'development.'
> But after all, there really are an awful lot of poor, sick,
> hungry people out there. What's to be done about it? If
> 'development' isn't the answer, then what is? ❞
>
> James Ferguson, *The Anti-Politics Machine: "Development," Depoliticization, and Bureaucratic Power in Lesotho*

been criticized for not examining the variety of experiences that development workers have and their competing interpretations of the projects on which they work.

It is also possible to argue that Ferguson's book has become outdated. Development priorities, policies, and practices have changed significantly since the 1980s. At the time when Ferguson was carrying out his fieldwork in the early 1980s, non-governmental organizations* and neoliberal* philosophies were just starting to emerge as key elements within development. In addition, development agencies have more recently started to incorporate an analysis of local politics into their planning and decision-making. This reduces the need for Ferguson's argument that development institutions ignore the political factors that contribute to the experience of poverty. The depth of these changes is, however, in dispute.[1]

Future Directions

Ferguson's provision of a powerful framework for exploring development interventions will continue to have relevance for anyone engaged in studying development. The question for many remains how to apply the insights of Ferguson and the postdevelopment* theorists he inspires to practical work that addresses the political dimensions of poverty and inequality. This refers both to applied work within development institutions and to work outside these institutions.

This question of how to apply Ferguson's ideas on a practical level has been asked repeatedly since *The Anti-Politics Machine* was published in 1990. It was central to the book *Anthropology, Development and the Post-modern Challenge* (1996) by the British anthropologists Katy Gardner* and David Lewis.*[2] The American anthropologist Mark Schuller* offers insightful suggestions in the afterword to his book *Killing with Kindness.* This book examines the role of international aid and non-governmental organizations in Haiti.[3] Schuller suggests that making changes to funding could make the biggest difference when it comes to addressing poverty. Funding for bilateral* government aid organizations and non-governmental organizations is tied to the political agendas of the donors. Schuller argues that if funding is untied from these political agendas, it would allow development organizations and development workers to work in a different way: "accompanying," rather than directing the people who are claiming the right to development and overall well-being.[4]

Summary

The Anti-Politics Machine is an important contribution to the study of development interventions. Ferguson was interested in the ideas of the French philosopher Michel Foucault about how knowledge is created and used in relationship to the exercise of power. Ferguson's originality lay in applying these ideas to the field of development. Ferguson argues that development institutions produce their own kind of discourse. These articulate a specific structure of "knowledge" about poor countries. But this formulaic style of knowledge creates unintended effects when it is translated into actual development projects. There are two key unintended effects:

- The extension of state control
- The depoliticization of poverty (the process by which politics is not understood as a central factor in creating and perpetuating poverty and inequality).

Anthropologists studying development have followed Ferguson in approaching development in a way that is conscious of how development knowledge is constituted and applied. But they question Ferguson's depiction of development institutions as homogenous entities. This has led to an increase in long-term research into variation in development. This research explores the variety of development organizations, their ideas about development, and what actually occurs within development interventions. It is likely that Ferguson will continue to be highly regarded and to provide inspiration for ongoing critical studies of international development institutions and projects.

NOTES

1   Laura Routley and David Hulme, "Donors, Development Agencies and the Use of Political Economic Analysis: Getting to Grips with the Politics of Development?," ESID Working Paper No. 19 (Manchester: University of Manchester, 2013).

2   Katy Gardner and David Lewis, *Anthropology, Development and the Post-Modern Challenge* (London: Pluto Press, 1996). See also, Andrew McGregor, "New Possibilities? Shifts in Post-Development Theory and Practice," *Geography Compass* 3, no. 5 (2009): 1688–1702.

3   Mark Schuller, *Killing with Kindness: Haiti, International Aid, and NGOs* (New Brunswick, NJ: Rutgers University Press, 2012).

4   Schuller, *Killing with Kindness*, 188–194.

GLOSSARY

GLOSSARY OF TERMS

Anthropology: the systematic study of humankind, particularly its beliefs and practices.

Authoritarian: a term describing a government whose intrusive authority restricts the freedoms of its citizens.

Basotho: the ethnic group that makes up most of the population of Lesotho.

Basotho National Party: a political party in Lesotho. Its political candidates held the office of prime minister from Lesotho's independence in 1966 until 1986. This leadership was, however, contested in the 1970 elections by the Basotho Congress Party, at which point the BNP declared a state of emergency. Elections were not held again until 1993.

Bilateral aid: refers to aid in the form of various types of resources such as monetary, technological, or military, given from one country to another.

Canadian International Development Agency (CIDA): the Canadian aid agency distributing bilateral aid to "developing" countries.

Capitalism: a social and economic system in which trade and industry are held in private hands and operated for the sake of private profit.

Colonialism: the practice of taking economic and political control over another country or territory.

Cultural Anthropology: the cross-cultural study of human behavior and thought.

Depoliticization: a term to describe the process by which the discourse concerning development serves to deny the political causes of and solutions to poverty.

Development: a system of directed social and economic change, through non-governmental organizations, bilateral aid organizations, and multilateral aid organizations.

Discourse: a complex concept with a variety of meanings. Ferguson uses the term in the sense of a codified form of language that is used in a given field of intellectual inquiry or social practice, and prescribes "acceptable statements and utterances" in that field (Ferguson, *The Anti-Politics Machine*, 18).

Ethnography: the study of people and cultures.

Feminism: the movement for equality between men and women; feminism has inspired many new theoretical advances and methods of analysis in anthropology, with an emphasis on reducing male bias.

Foucauldian: in the style of the work of the influential French social philosopher and historian Michel Foucault.

Governmentality: a concept originally developed by Michel Foucault that can be defined as the "art of government"—the body of institutions and methods that enable the government of a population. Ferguson uses it in a different sense: of a principle articulated by development discourse according to which a national economy is assumed to be "almost perfectly responsive to national government policy."

Lesotho: a country of about 30,000 square kilometers surrounded by the Republic of South Africa. It gained independence from Britain in 1966.

Multilateral aid: aid, given in the form of monetary or technological assistance, and distributed through institutions that collect resources from member countries.

Neoliberalism: an economic and political philosophy that promotes economic liberalization, deregulation, and privatization as the best way to further economic growth and social welfare.

Neo-Marxism: a category for twentieth-century approaches building on the work of Karl Marx (1818–83), a German philosopher and economist whose works such as *The Communist Manifesto* and *Capital: Critique of Political Economy* provided the foundations for a critical understanding of capitalism.

Non-governmental organizations (NGOs): not-for-profit organizations; although not part of a government, NGOs may be funded by governments (as well as by private individuals, businesses, and foundations).

Participant observation: an anthropological technique in which anthropologists take part in the daily lives of research participants.

Political economy approaches: approaches aimed at connecting anthropological fieldwork in specific communities or regions with an examination of larger, regional or global political and economic systems.

Postcolonial: the period following colonial rule, i.e. when a nation has gained its independence.

Postdevelopment literature: a set of literature generally understood as rejecting development as an ethical solution to poverty and inequality, and making calls for alternative strategies outside development.

Poststructuralism: a term used to describe a variety of critiques of the analytical approach to culture known as structuralism. Poststructuralists are critical of claims to objectivity and scientific neutrality, emphasizing instead the plurality of meaning in different historical and cultural contexts.

Structuralism: a set of theories arguing that the same underlying units of culture can be found in all societies, despite their more noticeable diversity, and that these can be identified through an objective analysis.

Structural functionalism: a set of theories arguing that institutions in society function to maintain group cohesion and cultural reproduction.

Subsistence agriculture: a farming strategy where only enough food is produced to fulfill the needs of a small group.

Sustainable Development Goals: international development goals set out in the United Nations Conference on Sustainable Development in 2012. These goals are an extension of the Millennial Declaration in 2000 for reducing poverty, hunger, child mortality, and disease, while ensuring universal access to education and gender equality. The SDG added the goals of addressing climate change and promoting sustainable development, consumption, and production.

Third World: a Western-centric term for countries that were not allied with either the Western Bloc or the Eastern Bloc during the Cold War. It is used to refer to developing nations in Africa, Asia and Latin America.

United Nations: an international body with its headquarters in New York founded in 1945 in order to promote cooperation and secure peace between the nations of the world.

United States Agency for International Development (USAID): the United States's aid agency distributing bilateral aid to "developing" countries.

World Bank: a multilateral aid institution that provides loans and advice to "developing" countries.

World-system and dependency theories: a set of theories that explain the unequal development of economies by their integration into a capitalist world order in which the wealthy "core" economies extract resources from the poor "peripheral" economies, thus keeping them in a state of dependency and underdevelopment.

PEOPLE MENTIONED IN THE TEXT

Paul Bohannan (1920–2007) was an American anthropologist who taught at Oxford University, Princeton University, Northwestern University, and the University of California, Santa Barbara. He was most known for his research on the Tiv people in Nigeria.

David Brokensha (b. 1923) is a South African anthropologist of Africa, development, and environment. He is a professor emeritus at the University of California in Santa Barbara.

Bram Büscher (b. 1977) is a Dutch anthropologist and political scientist whose work focuses on the links between neoliberalism and trans-frontier conservation in southern Africa. He is currently the chair of the Sociology of Development and Change group at Wageningen University.

Emma Crewe is an anthropologist, currently a professorial research associate at the School for Oriental and African Studies in London. Her work has included examining the politics of aid.

William Easterly (b. 1957) is an American economist working on economic growth and development. He is a professor at New York University and the codirector of NYU's Development Research Institute.

Arturo Escobar (b. 1952) is a Colombian American anthropologist who contributed especially to postdevelopment theory and political ecology. His best-known work is *Encountering Development: The Making and Unmaking of the Third World*. He is currently the Kenan Distinguished Professor of Anthropology at the University of North Carolina in Chapel Hill.

Michel Foucault (1926–84) was a French philosopher who wrote about the nature of power, its relationships with knowledge, and its exercise through a range of social institutions. His key works include *The Archaeology of Knowledge* and *Discipline and Punish: The Birth of the Prison.*

Katy Gardner (b. 1964) is a British anthropologist currently a professor at the London School of Economics. In her research, she focuses on migration and economic change in Bangladesh and its transnational communities in the UK.

Andre Gunder Frank (1929–2005) was a German American social scientist. He is considered to be both a dependency theorist and world-systems theorist in his work about employed dependency theories, and world-system theories in his work on the global political economy.

Akhil Gupta (b. 1959) is an Indian American anthropologist of the state and development, especially in the Indian context. He is a professor of anthropology at the University of California in Los Angeles.

Elizabeth Harrison is an anthropologist at the University of Sussex in the UK. She is currently the head of the department of international development. Her research includes examining the politics of aid.

David Lewis is the head of the social policy and development department at the London School of Economics. His work explores non-governmental organizations and their role in development.

Norman Long is a British anthropologist closely associated with "actor-oriented" approaches to international development. He is currently an emeritus professor of the sociology of development at Wageningen University in the Netherlands.

Liisa Malkki is a professor of cultural anthropology at Stanford University. Her best-known work is *Purity and Exile: Violence, Memory, and National Cosmology among Hutu Refugees in Tanzania*.

Sally Falk Moore (b. 1924) is a legal anthropologist and professor emerita at Harvard University. She undertook her major fieldwork in Tanzania.

David Mosse is a British anthropologist whose work focuses on development, environment, and religion in South Asia. His major contribution to the anthropology of development is *Cultivating Development: An Ethnography of Aid Policy and Practice*. He is presently a professor at the School for Oriental and African Studies in London.

Tania Murray Li (b. 1959) is a Canadian anthropologist whose more recent work focuses on the economy, environment, and development in Indonesia. She is currently a professor of anthropology at the University of Toronto.

Alexander F. Robertson (b. 1942) is a Scottish American anthropologist whose work focuses on family, greed, growth, and development. He is currently an honorary professor of social anthropology at Edinburgh University.

Walter Rodney (1942–80) was a Guyanese historian and political activist. He is best known for his book, *How Europe Underdeveloped Africa*, where he argued that European colonialism explicitly exploited the resources of their African colonies. This contributed to the contemporary "underdevelopment" of African countries.

Jeffrey D. Sachs (b. 1954) is an American economist who has become known for his role as an adviser to the governments of transitional economies in Eastern Europe and elsewhere. More recently, he has been concerned with topics such as development, sustainability, and poverty alleviation.

Jean-Pierre Olivier de Sardan (b. 1941) is a French anthropologist of politics, development, and social change in Africa. Some of his works, including *Anthropology and Development: Understanding Contemporary Social Change*, have been translated into English.

Mark Schuller is an American anthropologist at Northern Illinois University. His work examines the role of humanitarian aid and NGOs in Haiti.

Harry S. Truman (1884–1972) was the 33rd president of the United States, in office from 1945 to 1953.

Pieter de Vries (b. 1958) is a member of the Rural Development Sociology Group at the Wageningen University in the Netherlands. His work focuses on development, corruption, and politics in Latin America.

Max Weber (1864–1920) was a German social scientist. His studies focused on the relationship between individuals and action, and argued that generalized abstractions are "ideal-types," to which social reality never exactly matches.

Gavin Williams (b. 1943) is an emeritus fellow at St Peter's College, Oxford. He has published on land and agricultural reform and international development in Africa.

WORKS CITED

WORKS CITED

Brokensha, David, D. M. Warren, and Oswald Werner, eds. *Indigenous Knowledge Systems and Development*. Lanham, MD: University Press of America, 1980.

Büscher, Bram. "Anti-Politics as Political Strategy: Neoliberalism and Transfrontier Conservation in Southern Africa." *Development and Change* 41, no. 1 (2010): 29–51.

Cooper, Frederick. "The Anti-Politics Machine: 'Development,' Depoliticization, and Bureaucratic Power in Lesotho." *Journal of Southern African Studies* 16, no. 4 (1990), 771–4.

Crewe, Emma, and Elizabeth Harrison. *Whose Development? An Ethnography of Aid*. London: Zed Books, 1998.

Crewe, Emma, and Richard Axelby. *Anthropology and Development: Culture, Morality and Politics in a Globalised World*. Cambridge: Cambridge University Press, 2012.

De Sardan, Jean-Pierre Olivier. *Anthropology and Development: Understanding Contemporary Social Change*. London: Zed Books, 2005.

De Vries, Pieter. "Don't Compromise Your Desire for Development! A Lacanian/Deleuzian Rethinking of the Anti-Politics Machine." *Third World Quarterly* 28, no. 1 (2007): 25–43.

"A Research Journey: On Actors, Concepts and the Text." In *Battlefields of Knowledge: The Interlocking of Theory and Practice in Social Research and Development*, edited by Norman Long and Ann Long, 47–84. London: Routledge, 1992.

Easterly, William. *The White Man's Burden: Why the West's Efforts to Aid the Rest Have Done So Much Ill and So Little Good*. New York: Penguin, 2006.

Escobar, Arturo. "The Anti-Politics Machine: 'Development,' Depoliticization, and Bureaucratic Power in Lesotho." *American Ethnologist* 18, no. 3, Representations of Europe: Transforming State, Society, and Identity (1991), 618.

"Discourse and Power in Development: Michel Foucault and the Relevance of his Work to the Third World." *Alternatives* 10, no. 3 (1984): 377–400.

Encountering Development: The Making and Unmaking of the Third World. Princeton: Princeton University Press, 2012.

"Imagining a post-development era? Critical thought, development and social movements." *Social Text* 31–2 (1992): 20–56.

Ferguson, James. "Anthropology and Its Evil Twin: 'Development' in the Constitution of a Discipline." In *International Development and the Social Sciences: Essays on the History and Politics of Knowledge*, edited by Frederick Cooper and Randall Packard, 150–175. Berkeley: University of California Press, 1997.

The Anti-Politics Machine: "Development," Depoliticization, and Bureaucratic Power in Lesotho. Minneapolis, MN: University of Minnesota Press, 1994.

The Anti-Politics Machine: a Panel Review of James Ferguson's Book, with a Rejoinder by the Author. Roma: National University of Lesotho, 1992.

"Discourse, Knowledge, and Structural Production in the 'Development' Industry: An Anthropological Study of a Rural Development Project in Lesotho." PhD diss., Harvard University, 1985.

Expectations of Modernity: Myths and Meanings of Urban Life on the Zambian Copperbelt. Berkeley: University of California Press, 1999.

Give a Man a Fish: Reflections on the New Politics of Distribution. Duke University Press, 2015.

Global Shadows: Africa in the Neoliberal World Order. Durham and London: Duke University Press, 2006.

Ferguson, James, and Akhil Gupta, eds. *Anthropological Locations: Boundaries and Grounds of a Field Science.* Berkeley, CA: University of California Press, 1997.

Culture, Power, Place: Explorations in Critical Anthropology. London: Duke University Press, 1997.

Foucault, Michel. *Discipline and Punish: The Birth of the Prison*. Translated by A. Sheridan. Harmondsworth: Penguin, 1979.

"Governmentality." In *The Foucault Effect: Studies in Governmentality with Two Lectures by and an Interview with Michel Foucault,* edited by Graham Burchell, Colin Gordon and Peter Miller, 87–104. Chicago: Chicago University Press, 1991.

Frank, Andre Gunder. *Latin America: Underdevelopment or Revolution*. New York: Monthly Review Press, 1969.

Gardner, Katy, and David Lewis. *Anthropology, Development and the Post-Modern Challenge.* London: Pluto Press, 1996.

Geertz, Clifford. *The Interpretation of Cultures: Selected Essays*. Basic Books, 1973.

Grillo, Ralph D., and Roderick L. Stirrat, eds. *Discourses of Development: Anthropological Perspectives*. Oxford and New York: Berg, 1997.

Humanity Journal. "Interview with James Ferguson, Pt 1: Development as Swarming State Power." Accessed September 16, 2015. http://humanityjournal. org/blog/humanity-interview-with-james-ferguson-pt-1-development-as-swarming-state-power/.

Long, Norman. *Development Sociology: Actor Perspectives*. London and New York: Routledge, 2003.

Long, Norman and Alberto Arce, eds. *Anthropology, Development, and Modernities: Exploring Discourses, Counter-tendencies, and Violence*. London and New York: Routledge, 2000.

Long, Norman and Ann Long, eds. *Battlefields of Knowledge: The Interlocking of Theory and Practice in Social Research and Development*. London: Routledge, 1992.

McGregor, Andrew. "New Possibilities? Shifts in Post-Development Theory and Practice." *Geography Compass* 3, no. 5 (2009): 1688–1702.

Mosse, David. *Cultivating Development: An Ethnography of Aid Policy and Practice*. London: Pluto, 2005.

Murray, Colin. *Families Divided: The Impact of Migrant Labour in Lesotho*. New York: Cambridge University Press, 1981.

Murray Li, Tania. "Compromising power: Development, Culture, and Rule in Indonesia." *Cultural Anthropology* 14, no. 3 (1999), 295–322.

The Will to Improve: Governmentality, Development, and the Practice of Politics. Durham: Duke University Press, 2007.

Nederveen Pieterse, Jan. "My Paradigm or Yours? Alternative Development, Post-Development, Reflexive Development." *Development and Change* 29, no. 2 (1998): 343–73.

Polar. "Interview with James Ferguson and Akhil Gupta." Accessed September 16, 2015. http://www.polaronline.org/2012/04/15/james-ferguson-and-akhil-gupta/.

Robertson, Alexander F. "*The Anti-Politics Machine: 'Development,' Depoliticization, and Bureaucratic Power in Lesotho* by James Ferguson." *Journal of International Development* 4, no. 3 (1992): 337–40.

People and the State: An Anthropology of Planned Development. Cambridge: Cambridge University Press, 1984.

Rodney, Walter. *How Europe Underdeveloped Africa*. London. Bogle-L'ouverture Publications, 1972.

Routley, Laura, and David Hulme. "Donors, Development Agencies and the Use of Political Economic Analysis: Getting to Grips with the Politics of Development?" ESID Working Paper No. 19. Manchester: University of Manchester, 2013.

Schuller, Mark. *Killing with Kindness: Haiti, International Aid, and NGOs*. New Brunswisk, NJ: Rutgers University Press, 2012.

Theory Talks. "Theory Talk #34: James Ferguson on Modernity, Development, and Reading Foucault in Lesotho." Accessed September 16, 2015. http://www.theory-talks.org/2009/11/theory-talk-34.html.

World Bank. *Lesotho: A Development Challenge*. Washington, DC: World Bank, 1975.

World Bank. "Overview of Poverty." Accessed September 16, 2015. http://www.worldbank.org/en/topic/poverty/overview.

THE MACAT LIBRARY
BY DISCIPLINE

AFRICANA STUDIES

Chinua Achebe's *An Image of Africa: Racism in Conrad's Heart of Darkness*
W. E. B. Du Bois's *The Souls of Black Folk*
Zora Neale Huston's *Characteristics of Negro Expression*
Martin Luther King Jr's *Why We Can't Wait*
Toni Morrison's *Playing in the Dark: Whiteness in the American Literary Imagination*

ANTHROPOLOGY

Arjun Appadurai's *Modernity at Large: Cultural Dimensions of Globalisation*
Philippe Ariès's *Centuries of Childhood*
Franz Boas's *Race, Language and Culture*
Kim Chan & Renée Mauborgne's *Blue Ocean Strategy*
Jared Diamond's *Guns, Germs & Steel: the Fate of Human Societies*
Jared Diamond's *Collapse: How Societies Choose to Fail or Survive*
E. E. Evans-Pritchard's *Witchcraft, Oracles and Magic Among the Azande*
James Ferguson's *The Anti-Politics Machine*
Clifford Geertz's *The Interpretation of Cultures*
David Graeber's *Debt: the First 5000 Years*
Karen Ho's *Liquidated: An Ethnography of Wall Street*
Geert Hofstede's *Culture's Consequences: Comparing Values, Behaviors, Institutes and Organizations across Nations*
Claude Lévi-Strauss's *Structural Anthropology*
Jay Macleod's *Ain't No Makin' It: Aspirations and Attainment in a Low-Income Neighborhood*
Saba Mahmood's *The Politics of Piety: The Islamic Revival and the Feminist Subjec*t
Marcel Mauss's *The Gift*

BUSINESS

Jean Lave & Etienne Wenger's *Situated Learning*
Theodore Levitt's *Marketing Myopia*
Burton G. Malkiel's *A Random Walk Down Wall Street*
Douglas McGregor's *The Human Side of Enterprise*
Michael Porter's *Competitive Strategy: Creating and Sustaining Superior Performance*
John Kotter's *Leading Change*
C. K. Prahalad & Gary Hamel's *The Core Competence of the Corporation*

CRIMINOLOGY

Michelle Alexander's *The New Jim Crow: Mass Incarceration in the Age of Colorblindness*
Michael R. Gottfredson & Travis Hirschi's *A General Theory of Crime*
Richard Herrnstein & Charles A. Murray's *The Bell Curve: Intelligence and Class Structure in American Life*
Elizabeth Loftus's *Eyewitness Testimony*
Jay Macleod's *Ain't No Makin' It: Aspirations and Attainment in a Low-Income Neighborhood*
Philip Zimbardo's *The Lucifer Effect*

ECONOMICS

Janet Abu-Lughod's *Before European Hegemony*
Ha-Joon Chang's *Kicking Away the Ladder*
David Brion Davis's *The Problem of Slavery in the Age of Revolution*
Milton Friedman's *The Role of Monetary Policy*
Milton Friedman's *Capitalism and Freedom*
David Graeber's *Debt: the First 5000 Years*
Friedrich Hayek's *The Road to Serfdom*
Karen Ho's *Liquidated: An Ethnography of Wall Street*

John Maynard Keynes's *The General Theory of Employment, Interest and Money*
Charles P. Kindleberger's *Manias, Panics and Crashes*
Robert Lucas's *Why Doesn't Capital Flow from Rich to Poor Countries?*
Burton G. Malkiel's *A Random Walk Down Wall Street*
Thomas Robert Malthus's *An Essay on the Principle of Population*
Karl Marx's *Capital*
Thomas Piketty's *Capital in the Twenty-First Century*
Amartya Sen's *Development as Freedom*
Adam Smith's *The Wealth of Nations*
Nassim Nicholas Taleb's *The Black Swan: The Impact of the Highly Improbable*
Amos Tversky's & Daniel Kahneman's *Judgment under Uncertainty: Heuristics and Biases*
Mahbub Ul Haq's *Reflections on Human Development*
Max Weber's *The Protestant Ethic and the Spirit of Capitalism*

FEMINISM AND GENDER STUDIES

Judith Butler's *Gender Trouble*
Simone De Beauvoir's *The Second Sex*
Michel Foucault's *History of Sexuality*
Betty Friedan's *The Feminine Mystique*
Saba Mahmood's *The Politics of Piety: The Islamic Revival and the Feminist Subject*
Joan Wallach Scott's *Gender and the Politics of History*
Mary Wollstonecraft's *A Vindication of the Rights of Woman*
Virginia Woolf's *A Room of One's Own*

GEOGRAPHY

The Brundtland Report's *Our Common Future*
Rachel Carson's *Silent Spring*
Charles Darwin's *On the Origin of Species*
James Ferguson's *The Anti-Politics Machine*
Jane Jacobs's *The Death and Life of Great American Cities*
James Lovelock's *Gaia: A New Look at Life on Earth*
Amartya Sen's *Development as Freedom*
Mathis Wackernagel & William Rees's *Our Ecological Footprint*

HISTORY

Janet Abu-Lughod's *Before European Hegemony*
Benedict Anderson's *Imagined Communities*
Bernard Bailyn's *The Ideological Origins of the American Revolution*
Hanna Batatu's *The Old Social Classes And The Revolutionary Movements Of Iraq*
Christopher Browning's *Ordinary Men: Reserve Police Batallion 101 and the Final Solution in Poland*
Edmund Burke's *Reflections on the Revolution in France*
William Cronon's *Nature's Metropolis: Chicago And The Great West*
Alfred W. Crosby's *The Columbian Exchange*
Hamid Dabashi's *Iran: A People Interrupted*
David Brion Davis's *The Problem of Slavery in the Age of Revolution*
Nathalie Zemon Davis's *The Return of Martin Guerre*
Jared Diamond's *Guns, Germs & Steel: the Fate of Human Societies*
Frank Dikotter's *Mao's Great Famine*
John W Dower's *War Without Mercy: Race And Power In The Pacific War*
W. E. B. Du Bois's *The Souls of Black Folk*
Richard J. Evans's *In Defence of History*
Lucien Febvre's *The Problem of Unbelief in the 16th Century*
Sheila Fitzpatrick's *Everyday Stalinism*

Eric Foner's *Reconstruction: America's Unfinished Revolution, 1863-1877*
Michel Foucault's *Discipline and Punish*
Michel Foucault's *History of Sexuality*
Francis Fukuyama's *The End of History and the Last Man*
John Lewis Gaddis's *We Now Know: Rethinking Cold War History*
Ernest Gellner's *Nations and Nationalism*
Eugene Genovese's *Roll, Jordan, Roll: The World the Slaves Made*
Carlo Ginzburg's *The Night Battles*
Daniel Goldhagen's *Hitler's Willing Executioners*
Jack Goldstone's *Revolution and Rebellion in the Early Modern World*
Antonio Gramsci's *The Prison Notebooks*
Alexander Hamilton, John Jay & James Madison's *The Federalist Papers*
Christopher Hill's *The World Turned Upside Down*
Carole Hillenbrand's *The Crusades: Islamic Perspectives*
Thomas Hobbes's *Leviathan*
Eric Hobsbawm's *The Age Of Revolution*
John A. Hobson's *Imperialism: A Study*
Albert Hourani's *History of the Arab Peoples*
Samuel P. Huntington's *The Clash of Civilizations and the Remaking of World Order*
C. L. R. James's *The Black Jacobins*
Tony Judt's *Postwar: A History of Europe Since 1945*
Ernst Kantorowicz's *The King's Two Bodies: A Study in Medieval Political Theology*
Paul Kennedy's *The Rise and Fall of the Great Powers*
Ian Kershaw's *The "Hitler Myth": Image and Reality in the Third Reich*
John Maynard Keynes's *The General Theory of Employment, Interest and Money*
Charles P. Kindleberger's *Manias, Panics and Crashes*
Martin Luther King Jr's *Why We Can't Wait*
Henry Kissinger's *World Order: Reflections on the Character of Nations and the Course of History*
Thomas Kuhn's *The Structure of Scientific Revolutions*
Georges Lefebvre's *The Coming of the French Revolution*
John Locke's *Two Treatises of Government*
Niccolò Machiavelli's *The Prince*
Thomas Robert Malthus's *An Essay on the Principle of Population*
Mahmood Mamdani's *Citizen and Subject: Contemporary Africa And The Legacy Of Late Colonialism*
Karl Marx's *Capital*
Stanley Milgram's *Obedience to Authority*
John Stuart Mill's *On Liberty*
Thomas Paine's *Common Sense*
Thomas Paine's *Rights of Man*
Geoffrey Parker's *Global Crisis: War, Climate Change and Catastrophe in the Seventeenth Century*
Jonathan Riley-Smith's *The First Crusade and the Idea of Crusading*
Jean-Jacques Rousseau's *The Social Contract*
Joan Wallach Scott's *Gender and the Politics of History*
Theda Skocpol's *States and Social Revolutions*
Adam Smith's *The Wealth of Nations*
Timothy Snyder's *Bloodlands: Europe Between Hitler and Stalin*
Sun Tzu's *The Art of War*
Keith Thomas's *Religion and the Decline of Magic*
Thucydides's *The History of the Peloponnesian War*
Frederick Jackson Turner's *The Significance of the Frontier in American History*
Odd Arne Westad's *The Global Cold War: Third World Interventions And The Making Of Our Times*

The Macat Library By Discipline

LITERATURE

Chinua Achebe's *An Image of Africa: Racism in Conrad's Heart of Darkness*
Roland Barthes's *Mythologies*
Homi K. Bhabha's *The Location of Culture*
Judith Butler's *Gender Trouble*
Simone De Beauvoir's *The Second Sex*
Ferdinand De Saussure's *Course in General Linguistics*
T. S. Eliot's *The Sacred Wood: Essays on Poetry and Criticism*
Zora Neale Huston's *Characteristics of Negro Expression*
Toni Morrison's *Playing in the Dark: Whiteness in the American Literary Imagination*
Edward Said's *Orientalism*
Gayatri Chakravorty Spivak's *Can the Subaltern Speak?*
Mary Wollstonecraft's *A Vindication of the Rights of Women*
Virginia Woolf's *A Room of One's Own*

PHILOSOPHY

Elizabeth Anscombe's *Modern Moral Philosophy*
Hannah Arendt's *The Human Condition*
Aristotle's *Metaphysics*
Aristotle's *Nicomachean Ethics*
Edmund Gettier's *Is Justified True Belief Knowledge?*
Georg Wilhelm Friedrich Hegel's *Phenomenology of Spirit*
David Hume's *Dialogues Concerning Natural Religion*
David Hume's *The Enquiry for Human Understanding*
Immanuel Kant's *Religion within the Boundaries of Mere Reason*
Immanuel Kant's *Critique of Pure Reason*
Søren Kierkegaard's *The Sickness Unto Death*
Søren Kierkegaard's *Fear and Trembling*
C. S. Lewis's *The Abolition of Man*
Alasdair MacIntyre's *After Virtue*
Marcus Aurelius's *Meditations*
Friedrich Nietzsche's *On the Genealogy of Morality*
Friedrich Nietzsche's *Beyond Good and Evil*
Plato's *Republic*
Plato's *Symposium*
Jean-Jacques Rousseau's *The Social Contract*
Gilbert Ryle's *The Concept of Mind*
Baruch Spinoza's *Ethics*
Sun Tzu's *The Art of War*
Ludwig Wittgenstein's *Philosophical Investigations*

POLITICS

Benedict Anderson's *Imagined Communities*
Aristotle's *Politics*
Bernard Bailyn's *The Ideological Origins of the American Revolution*
Edmund Burke's *Reflections on the Revolution in France*
John C. Calhoun's *A Disquisition on Government*
Ha-Joon Chang's *Kicking Away the Ladder*
Hamid Dabashi's *Iran: A People Interrupted*
Hamid Dabashi's *Theology of Discontent: The Ideological Foundation of the Islamic Revolution in Iran*
Robert Dahl's *Democracy and its Critics*
Robert Dahl's *Who Governs?*
David Brion Davis's *The Problem of Slavery in the Age of Revolution*

Alexis De Tocqueville's *Democracy in America*
James Ferguson's *The Anti-Politics Machine*
Frank Dikotter's *Mao's Great Famine*
Sheila Fitzpatrick's *Everyday Stalinism*
Eric Foner's *Reconstruction: America's Unfinished Revolution, 1863-1877*
Milton Friedman's *Capitalism and Freedom*
Francis Fukuyama's *The End of History and the Last Man*
John Lewis Gaddis's *We Now Know: Rethinking Cold War History*
Ernest Gellner's *Nations and Nationalism*
David Graeber's *Debt: the First 5000 Years*
Antonio Gramsci's *The Prison Notebooks*
Alexander Hamilton, John Jay & James Madison's *The Federalist Papers*
Friedrich Hayek's *The Road to Serfdom*
Christopher Hill's *The World Turned Upside Down*
Thomas Hobbes's *Leviathan*
John A. Hobson's *Imperialism: A Study*
Samuel P. Huntington's *The Clash of Civilizations and the Remaking of World Order*
Tony Judt's *Postwar: A History of Europe Since 1945*
David C. Kang's *China Rising: Peace, Power and Order in East Asia*
Paul Kennedy's *The Rise and Fall of Great Powers*
Robert Keohane's *After Hegemony*
Martin Luther King Jr.'s *Why We Can't Wait*
Henry Kissinger's *World Order: Reflections on the Character of Nations and the Course of History*
John Locke's *Two Treatises of Government*
Niccolò Machiavelli's *The Prince*
Thomas Robert Malthus's *An Essay on the Principle of Population*
Mahmood Mamdani's *Citizen and Subject: Contemporary Africa And The Legacy Of Late Colonialism*
Karl Marx's *Capital*
John Stuart Mill's *On Liberty*
John Stuart Mill's *Utilitarianism*
Hans Morgenthau's *Politics Among Nations*
Thomas Paine's *Common Sense*
Thomas Paine's *Rights of Man*
Thomas Piketty's *Capital in the Twenty-First Century*
Robert D. Putman's *Bowling Alone*
John Rawls's *Theory of Justice*
Jean-Jacques Rousseau's *The Social Contract*
Theda Skocpol's *States and Social Revolutions*
Adam Smith's *The Wealth of Nations*
Sun Tzu's *The Art of War*
Henry David Thoreau's *Civil Disobedience*
Thucydides's *The History of the Peloponnesian War*
Kenneth Waltz's *Theory of International Politics*
Max Weber's *Politics as a Vocation*
Odd Arne Westad's *The Global Cold War: Third World Interventions And The Making Of Our Times*

POSTCOLONIAL STUDIES

Roland Barthes's *Mythologies*
Frantz Fanon's *Black Skin, White Masks*
Homi K. Bhabha's *The Location of Culture*
Gustavo Gutiérrez's *A Theology of Liberation*
Edward Said's *Orientalism*
Gayatri Chakravorty Spivak's *Can the Subaltern Speak?*

The Macat Library By Discipline

PSYCHOLOGY

Gordon Allport's *The Nature of Prejudice*
Alan Baddeley & Graham Hitch's *Aggression: A Social Learning Analysis*
Albert Bandura's *Aggression: A Social Learning Analysis*
Leon Festinger's *A Theory of Cognitive Dissonance*
Sigmund Freud's *The Interpretation of Dreams*
Betty Friedan's *The Feminine Mystique*
Michael R. Gottfredson & Travis Hirschi's *A General Theory of Crime*
Eric Hoffer's *The True Believer: Thoughts on the Nature of Mass Movements*
William James's *Principles of Psychology*
Elizabeth Loftus's *Eyewitness Testimony*
A. H. Maslow's *A Theory of Human Motivation*
Stanley Milgram's *Obedience to Authority*
Steven Pinker's *The Better Angels of Our Nature*
Oliver Sacks's *The Man Who Mistook His Wife For a Hat*
Richard Thaler & Cass Sunstein's *Nudge: Improving Decisions About Health, Wealth and Happiness*
Amos Tversky's *Judgment under Uncertainty: Heuristics and Biases*
Philip Zimbardo's *The Lucifer Effect*

SCIENCE

Rachel Carson's *Silent Spring*
William Cronon's *Nature's Metropolis: Chicago And The Great West*
Alfred W. Crosby's *The Columbian Exchange*
Charles Darwin's *On the Origin of Species*
Richard Dawkin's *The Selfish Gene*
Thomas Kuhn's *The Structure of Scientific Revolutions*
Geoffrey Parker's *Global Crisis: War, Climate Change and Catastrophe in the Seventeenth Century*
Mathis Wackernagel & William Rees's *Our Ecological Footprint*

SOCIOLOGY

Michelle Alexander's *The New Jim Crow: Mass Incarceration in the Age of Colorblindness*
Gordon Allport's *The Nature of Prejudice*
Albert Bandura's *Aggression: A Social Learning Analysis*
Hanna Batatu's *The Old Social Classes And The Revolutionary Movements Of Iraq*
Ha-Joon Chang's *Kicking Away the Ladder*
W. E. B. Du Bois's *The Souls of Black Folk*
Émile Durkheim's *On Suicide*
Frantz Fanon's *Black Skin, White Masks*
Frantz Fanon's *The Wretched of the Earth*
Eric Foner's *Reconstruction: America's Unfinished Revolution, 1863-1877*
Eugene Genovese's *Roll, Jordan, Roll: The World the Slaves Made*
Jack Goldstone's *Revolution and Rebellion in the Early Modern World*
Antonio Gramsci's *The Prison Notebooks*
Richard Herrnstein & Charles A Murray's *The Bell Curve: Intelligence and Class Structure in American Life*
Eric Hoffer's *The True Believer: Thoughts on the Nature of Mass Movements*
Jane Jacobs's *The Death and Life of Great American Cities*
Robert Lucas's *Why Doesn't Capital Flow from Rich to Poor Countries?*
Jay Macleod's *Ain't No Makin' It: Aspirations and Attainment in a Low Income Neighborhood*
Elaine May's *Homeward Bound: American Families in the Cold War Era*
Douglas McGregor's *The Human Side of Enterprise*
C. Wright Mills's *The Sociological Imagination*

Thomas Piketty's *Capital in the Twenty-First Century*
Robert D. Putman's *Bowling Alone*
David Riesman's *The Lonely Crowd: A Study of the Changing American Character*
Edward Said's *Orientalism*
Joan Wallach Scott's *Gender and the Politics of History*
Theda Skocpol's *States and Social Revolutions*
Max Weber's *The Protestant Ethic and the Spirit of Capitalism*

THEOLOGY

Augustine's *Confessions*
Benedict's *Rule of St Benedict*
Gustavo Gutiérrez's *A Theology of Liberation*
Carole Hillenbrand's *The Crusades: Islamic Perspectives*
David Hume's *Dialogues Concerning Natural Religion*
Immanuel Kant's *Religion within the Boundaries of Mere Reason*
Ernst Kantorowicz's *The King's Two Bodies: A Study in Medieval Political Theology*
Søren Kierkegaard's *The Sickness Unto Death*
C. S. Lewis's *The Abolition of Man*
Saba Mahmood's *The Politics of Piety: The Islamic Revival and the Feminist Subject*
Baruch Spinoza's *Ethics*
Keith Thomas's *Religion and the Decline of Magic*

COMING SOON

Chris Argyris's *The Individual and the Organisation*
Seyla Benhabib's *The Rights of Others*
Walter Benjamin's *The Work Of Art in the Age of Mechanical Reproduction*
John Berger's *Ways of Seeing*
Pierre Bourdieu's *Outline of a Theory of Practice*
Mary Douglas's *Purity and Danger*
Roland Dworkin's *Taking Rights Seriously*
James G. March's *Exploration and Exploitation in Organisational Learning*
Ikujiro Nonaka's *A Dynamic Theory of Organizational Knowledge Creation*
Griselda Pollock's *Vision and Difference*
Amartya Sen's *Inequality Re-Examined*
Susan Sontag's *On Photography*
Yasser Tabbaa's *The Transformation of Islamic Art*
Ludwig von Mises's *Theory of Money and Credit*

Macat Disciplines

Access the greatest ideas and thinkers across entire disciplines, including

AFRICANA STUDIES

Chinua Achebe's *An Image of Africa:
Racism in Conrad's Heart of Darkness*

W. E. B. Du Bois's *The Souls of Black Folk*

Zora Neale Hurston's *Characteristics of Negro Expression*

Martin Luther King Jr.'s *Why We Can't Wait*

Toni Morrison's *Playing in the Dark:
Whiteness in the American Literary Imagination*

Macat analyses are available from all good bookshops and libraries.

Access hundreds of analyses through one, multimedia tool.
Join free for one month **library.macat.com**

Macat Disciplines

Access the greatest ideas and thinkers across entire disciplines, including

FEMINISM, GENDER AND QUEER STUDIES

Simone De Beauvoir's
The Second Sex

Michel Foucault's
History of Sexuality

Betty Friedan's
The Feminine Mystique

Saba Mahmood's
*The Politics of Piety:
The Islamic Revival and
the Feminist Subject*

Joan Wallach Scott's
*Gender and the
Politics of History*

Mary Wollstonecraft's
*A Vindication of the
Rights of Woman*

Virginia Woolf's
A Room of One's Own

Judith Butler's
Gender Trouble

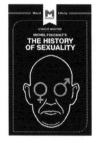

Macat analyses are available from all good bookshops and libraries.

Access hundreds of analyses through one, multimedia tool.
Join free for one month **library.macat.com**

Macat Disciplines

Access the greatest ideas and thinkers across entire disciplines, including

CRIMINOLOGY

Michelle Alexander's
*The New Jim Crow:
Mass Incarceration in the
Age of Colorblindness*

**Michael R. Gottfredson
& Travis Hirschi's**
A General Theory of Crime

Elizabeth Loftus's
Eyewitness Testimony

**Richard Herrnstein
& Charles A. Murray's**
*The Bell Curve: Intelligence and
Class Structure in American Life*

Jay Macleod's
*Ain't No Makin' It:
Aspirations and Attainment in a
Low-Income Neighborhood*

Philip Zimbardo's
The Lucifer Effect

Macat analyses are available from all good bookshops and libraries.

Access hundreds of analyses through one, multimedia tool.
Join free for one month **library.macat.com**

Macat Disciplines

Access the greatest ideas and thinkers across entire disciplines, including

INEQUALITY

Ha-Joon Chang's, *Kicking Away the Ladder*

David Graeber's, *Debt: The First 5000 Years*

Robert E. Lucas's, *Why Doesn't Capital Flow from Rich To Poor Countries?*

Thomas Piketty's, *Capital in the Twenty-First Century*

Amartya Sen's, *Inequality Re-Examined*

Mahbub Ul Haq's, *Reflections on Human Development*

Macat Disciplines

Access the greatest ideas and thinkers across entire disciplines, including

GLOBALIZATION

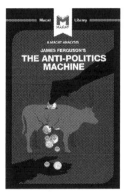

Arjun Appadurai's, *Modernity at Large: Cultural Dimensions of Globalisation*

James Ferguson's, *The Anti-Politics Machine*

Geert Hofstede's, *Culture's Consequences*

Amartya Sen's, *Development as Freedom*

Macat Disciplines

*Access the greatest ideas and thinkers
across entire disciplines, including*

THE FUTURE OF DEMOCRACY

Robert A. Dahl's, *Democracy and Its Critics*
Robert A. Dahl's, *Who Governs?*
Alexis De Toqueville's, *Democracy in America*
Niccolò Machiavelli's, *The Prince*
John Stuart Mill's, *On Liberty*
Robert D. Putnam's, *Bowling Alone*
Jean-Jacques Rousseau's, *The Social Contract*
Henry David Thoreau's, *Civil Disobedience*

Macat Disciplines

*Access the greatest ideas and thinkers
across entire disciplines, including*

TOTALITARIANISM

Sheila Fitzpatrick's, *Everyday Stalinism*
Ian Kershaw's, *The "Hitler Myth"*
Timothy Snyder's, *Bloodlands*

Macat analyses are available from all good bookshops and libraries.

Access hundreds of analyses through one, multimedia tool.
Join free for one month **library.macat.com**

Macat Pairs

Analyse historical and modern issues from opposite sides of an argument. Pairs include:

RACE AND IDENTITY

Zora Neale Hurston's
Characteristics of Negro Expression

Using material collected on anthropological expeditions to the South, Zora Neale Hurston explains how expression in African American culture in the early twentieth century departs from the art of white America. At the time, African American art was often criticized for copying white culture. For Hurston, this criticism misunderstood how art works. European tradition views art as something fixed. But Hurston describes a creative process that is alive, ever-changing, and largely improvisational. She maintains that African American art works through a process called 'mimicry'—where an imitated object or verbal pattern, for example, is reshaped and altered until it becomes something new, novel—and worthy of attention.

Frantz Fanon's
Black Skin, White Masks

Black Skin, White Masks offers a radical analysis of the psychological effects of colonization on the colonized.

Fanon witnessed the effects of colonization first hand both in his birthplace, Martinique, and again later in life when he worked as a psychiatrist in another French colony, Algeria. His text is uncompromising in form and argument. He dissects the dehumanizing effects of colonialism, arguing that it destroys the native sense of identity, forcing people to adapt to an alien set of values—including a core belief that they are inferior. This results in deep psychological trauma.

Fanon's work played a pivotal role in the civil rights movements of the 1960s.

Macat analyses are available from all good bookshops and libraries.

Access hundreds of analyses through one, multimedia tool.
Join free for one month **library.macat.com**

Macat Pairs

Analyse historical and modern issues from opposite sides of an argument. Pairs include:

HOW TO RUN AN ECONOMY

John Maynard Keynes's
The General Theory OF Employment, Interest and Money

Classical economics suggests that market economies are self-correcting in times of recession or depression, and tend toward full employment and output. But English economist John Maynard Keynes disagrees.

In his ground-breaking 1936 study *The General Theory*, Keynes argues that traditional economics has misunderstood the causes of unemployment. Employment is not determined by the price of labor; it is directly linked to demand. Keynes believes market economies are by nature unstable, and so require government intervention. Spurred on by the social catastrophe of the Great Depression of the 1930s, he sets out to revolutionize the way the world thinks

Milton Friedman's
The Role of Monetary Policy

Friedman's 1968 paper changed the course of economic theory. In just 17 pages, he demolished existing theory and outlined an effective alternate monetary policy designed to secure 'high employment, stable prices and rapid growth.'

Friedman demonstrated that monetary policy plays a vital role in broader economic stability and argued that economists got their monetary policy wrong in the 1950s and 1960s by misunderstanding the relationship between inflation and unemployment. Previous generations of economists had believed that governments could permanently decrease unemployment by permitting inflation—and vice versa. Friedman's most original contribution was to show that this supposed trade-off is an illusion that only works in the short term.

Macat analyses are available from all good bookshops and libraries.

Access hundreds of analyses through one, multimedia tool.
Join free for one month **library.macat.com**

Macat Pairs

Analyse historical and modern issues from opposite sides of an argument. Pairs include:

ARE WE FUNDAMENTALLY GOOD - OR BAD?

Steven Pinker's
The Better Angels of Our Nature

Stephen Pinker's gloriously optimistic 2011 book argues that, despite humanity's biological tendency toward violence, we are, in fact, less violent today than ever before. To prove his case, Pinker lays out pages of detailed statistical evidence. For him, much of the credit for the decline goes to the eighteenth-century Enlightenment movement, whose ideas of liberty, tolerance, and respect for the value of human life filtered down through society and affected how people thought. That psychological change led to behavioral change—and overall we became more peaceful. Critics countered that humanity could never overcome the biological urge toward violence; others argued that Pinker's statistics were flawed.

Philip Zimbardo's
The Lucifer Effect

Some psychologists believe those who commit cruelty are innately evil. Zimbardo disagrees. In *The Lucifer Effect*, he argues that sometimes good people do evil things simply because of the situations they find themselves in, citing many historical examples to illustrate his point. Zimbardo details his 1971 Stanford prison experiment, where ordinary volunteers playing guards in a mock prison rapidly became abusive. But he also describes the tortures committed by US army personnel in Iraq's Abu Ghraib prison in 2003—and how he himself testified in defence of one of those guards. committed by US army personnel in Iraq's Abu Ghraib prison in 2003—and how he himself testified in defence of one of those guards.

Macat analyses are available from all good bookshops and libraries.

Access hundreds of analyses through one, multimedia tool.
Join free for one month **library.macat.com**

Macat Pairs

Analyse historical and modern issues from opposite sides of an argument. Pairs include:

HOW WE RELATE TO EACH OTHER AND SOCIETY

Jean-Jacques Rousseau's
The Social Contract

Rousseau's famous work sets out the radical concept of the 'social contract': a give-and-take relationship between individual freedom and social order.

If people are free to do as they like, governed only by their own sense of justice, they are also vulnerable to chaos and violence. To avoid this, Rousseau proposes, they should agree to give up some freedom to benefit from the protection of social and political organization. But this deal is only just if societies are led by the collective needs and desires of the people, and able to control the private interests of individuals. For Rousseau, the only legitimate form of government is rule by the people.

Robert D. Putnam's
Bowling Alone

In *Bowling Alone*, Robert Putnam argues that Americans have become disconnected from one another and from the institutions of their common life, and investigates the consequences of this change.

Looking at a range of indicators, from membership in formal organizations to the number of invitations being extended to informal dinner parties, Putnam demonstrates that Americans are interacting less and creating less "social capital" – with potentially disastrous implications for their society.

It would be difficult to overstate the impact of *Bowling Alone*, one of the most frequently cited social science publications of the last half-century.

Printed in the United States
by Baker & Taylor Publisher Services